WHAT ARE YOU WORTH?

WHAT
ARE YOU
WORTH?

Edward M. Hallowell, M.D.
and William J. Grace, Jr.

WEIDENFELD & NICOLSON
NEW YORK

All opinions expressed in this book are strictly those of the authors themselves and are not to be viewed as representative of any institutions with which they are associated.

The characters in this book have been created for purposes of illustration only. Any resemblance to actual persons is entirely coincidental.

PUBLISHED BY WEIDENFELD & NICOLSON, NEW YORK
A DIVISION OF WHEATLAND CORPORATION
841 BROADWAY
NEW YORK, NEW YORK 10003-4793

PUBLISHED IN CANADA BY GENERAL PUBLISHING COMPANY, LTD.

LIBRARY OF CONGRESS CATALOGING-IN-PUBLICATION DATA

HALLOWELL, EDWARD M.
WHAT ARE YOU WORTH? / BY EDWARD M. HALLOWELL AND
WILLIAM GRACE. — 1ST ED.
P.   CM.
ISBN 1-55584-089-2
1. MONEY—PSYCHOLOGICAL ASPECTS.   I. GRACE, WILLIAM J.
II. TITLE.
HG222.3.H35 1989   88-14012
332.4'01'9—DC19   CIP

MANUFACTURED IN THE UNITED STATES OF AMERICA

THIS BOOK IS PRINTED ON ACID-FREE PAPER.

DESIGNED BY IRVING PERKINS ASSOCIATES

FIRST EDITION

1   3   5   7   9   10   8   6   4   2

For Sue and Ellen
—E.M.H.

For Valerie
—W.J.G.

We would like to acknowledge the generous assistance of the following people: Lyn and Tom Bliss, Phil Burnham, Eva Caira, Jon and Susan Galassi, Tom Gutheil, Jamie Hallowell, John Hallowell, John Herman, Harry Levinson, Peter Metz, Alex Packer, Susan Protter, John Ratey, Carol Rinzler, and Rafe Sagalyn.

Contents

Introduction

Ned Hallowell, a Harvard psychiatrist, and Bill Grace, a Merrill Lynch vice president, were exchanging anecdotes about their work one evening over dinner. The more the two old friends talked, the more Grace found himself saying, "What some of my clients really need is a good shrink to help them understand their anxieties about money," and the more Hallowell found himself saying, "What some of my patients really need is good financial advice to get them over their worries about money."

In the course of that evening, the idea for this book was born. What excited both Hallowell and Grace was combining practical financial advice with an explanation of how money affects people psychologically. Reading the book would be like having a financial adviser and a psychiatrist in the same room at the same time. If you complained, for instance, that you just couldn't keep yourself from overspending, the psychiatrist would point out the likely emotional causes and cures for your problem, and the financial expert would come up with a game plan that took into account your psychological makeup.

It is Hallowell and Grace's contention that most people make financial decisions on the basis of gut-level emotion instead of rational thought. This book, then, is first about understanding your feelings about money and then about gaining control of the money itself. It will help you if you fall into one or more of these traps:

—Never asking your employer for what you're really worth.
—Thinking money doesn't matter, then getting depressed when you don't have enough.
—Devoting all your energy to making big bucks, even though you know the money itself isn't really what you're after.
—Taking unnecessary financial risks, constantly flirting with financial ruin.
—Always passing up financial opportunities, and always regretting it.
—Giving control of your money to your spouse, even though you know he or she handles it foolishly.
—Putting off what you really want to do until "someday, when I have the money . . ."

When most of us think about our problems with money, we don't think at all. Instead, we shift into a state of anxiety that rapidly escalates until we change the subject or make a joke. Money is so charged with emotion, symbolizes so many things, that when we talk about it, especially with someone we're close to, it's almost impossible to do so rationally.

Consider David and Franny, a house-hunting married couple in their thirties who are discussing two houses they particularly like, one significantly more expensive than the other. The discussion soon deteriorates into a quarrel. David, who likes the more expensive house, accuses Franny of always being too cautious. Franny tells David he's so irresponsible about money that if it weren't for her they wouldn't have enough saved to make a down payment on an outhouse.

The reason Franny and David can't stay calm long enough

to talk about the merits of the two houses and reasonably assess how big a mortgage they can handle lies in the emotional meaning of money to each of them. Franny grew up poor, and money for her represents security. Even slightly overextending herself financially makes her feel frightened and insecure. David, on the other hand, grew up with rich but penny-pinching parents. To him the small house feels like more of the same.

Until David and Franny can examine these underlying issues and talk them through with mutual reassurance and understanding, they will remain stalemated, or, if they reach a solution, it will be the result of a power play by one of them. In their case, as in so many others, the actual money involved isn't the problem; the emotions surrounding it are.

The same is true of George, a forty-six-year-old bachelor who owns a small photography studio. The business is successful, but George has no savings or real estate. When his brother, an investment banker, offered to help him plan for financial security, George told his brother he was too busy to think about investments; his best bet, he said, was to spend all his energy on building up the business so that he could get really rich.

Again, George's problem isn't cerebral but emotional. Even the simple act of asking for help with money frightens him. Although he may have good reasons not to turn to his brother, he should be able to get advice from someone. Without careful planning, much of his hard work may be wasted. Some people don't plan because they grew up well taken care of financially and retain a fixed belief that it will always be that way. Others are unconsciously living out a life plan of self-destruction that includes financial hardship. Still others are too threatened by the anxiety that surrounds the topic to examine it at all.

The object of this book is to help you identify and analyze

the emotions that cloud your thinking—and adversely affect your actions—about money. Freud said of the purpose of psychoanalysis, "Where id was, there ego shall be." His goal was to harness our emotions so that we could be their master instead of their slave. We want to do the same for money.

The Meaning of Money

Money has no inherent meaning, no definitive form. It's a symbol, an agreed-upon unit of value, the financial equivalent of a unit of energy in physics. But unlike a volt or a calorie, this unit means different things to different people. To some it means freedom, to others security, to others power or self-esteem or love. The particular emotions you load onto money determine its meaning for you.

In Part One of this book, we'll show you how to determine which emotions you've chosen, where they came from, and how they affect your handling of money. First, think about the role money has played in your life. Did your parents use money to reward you for doing what they wanted? Did they give you money instead of attention? Were you taught about handling money, or were you told to leave it to Dad? Does money keep you in your job or marriage? Do you live beyond your means?

The Agreement

Once you have a better idea of what money means to you, you can determine and deal with your "agreement" with money. What do you want from money? What are you willing to do to get it?

Everyone strikes an agreement with money. Not everyone

knows what it is, which can lead to a lot of unhappiness. If, for instance, you wind up miserable in a high-paying job, that may be because your agreement with money was bogus. You may have asked money to do something money alone can't do: make you happy.

We tend to avoid assessing our agreement with money because that can force painful decisions. "I love being a teacher, but I also love fast cars and fine wine." Or, "I hate the track to partner, but it's the fastest way I know to make a lot of money." Or, "I will work extra hard so my wife won't have to work, which gives me an excuse to keep her at home so she can't compete with my career."

There are creative ways to deal with conflicts like these, but you won't be in an inventive frame of mind until you determine your agreement. Is it realistic, or is it based on magic?

Money Styles

People's personalities can be divided into certain types (the introvert and the extrovert, for instance); their styles of handling money can be distinguished in the same way. And a person's "money style" has more to do with his emotional makeup than with the immediate demands of reality.

In Part Two of this book, we'll show you how to determine your individual money style. We'll take you beyond the most obvious—your net worth or your annual income. You'll examine the little things you do every day. How much do you tip? How do you divide up a check with friends? How do you pay your bills? Do you risk a ticket in order to get a good parking place? If you're married, which of you handles the money? When was the last time you asked for a raise?

Once you understand the emotional components of money, you will see that it makes no sense to give the same advice to two people of different styles, even if they're both the same age and have the same income and goals. Part Two of the book will show you, through case histories, ways of dealing with money that will work for you. And you'll be able to match up your money style with a financial plan that fits it.

Part One

THE MEANINGS
OF MONEY

One

The Emotions
of Money

Why Money Makes You Anxious

Imagine yourself:

- —Asking for a raise.
- —Calculating whether you can afford a new house.
- —Setting a fee for your services face-to-face with a client.
- —Figuring out with your spouse where all your money went last year.
- —Paying your bills.
- —Discovering that a less competent colleague at work makes more than you do.
- —Asking a friend for a loan—or lending money to a friend and then collecting.

If you're like most people, you're feeling a little tense right now. The fact is, money makes almost all of us anxious. Of course, if you look behind money you'll find other issues— envy, aggression, and more—but the anxiety makes it hard to take that look.

People deal with this anxiety in many different ways. One way is simply to avoid the subject of money entirely. Another approach is just the opposite: to talk about virtually nothing else. People who take the latter route are constantly asking for or giving financial advice, boasting about making a killing or wailing about a big loss, worrying or prognosticating, in general never leaving the topic alone. Their anxiety is like that of an adolescent who has just discovered sex.

Often the anxiety we feel around money is self-destructive—when it comes to asking for a raise, for instance. Merely dealing with a boss on a day-to-day basis can be psychologically taxing, but when money is added to the mix the anxiety level can rise high enough to cloud our judgment or paralyze us. Anxiety can lead to flubbing the presentation or never asking for the raise at all.

Fee setting can offer another classic example of anxiety about money interfering with judgment. A consulting psychologist, hired by a corporation, "forgets" to set his fee. When he submits his bill at the end of the project, the company properly argues that they never knew it would be so high. You may be superbly competent, an expert in your field, but when it comes to asking for what you're worth the nervousness that accompanies the subject of money causes you to undervalue yourself. When there is an interaction between money and self-esteem there is often conflict and anxiety.

You can probably think of dozens of examples of money-related anxiety having hindered your rational behavior. Some of us, for instance, become so anxious when presented with an inflated bill that we are unable to argue about it effectively. People too eager to conclude a financial negotiation often shortchange themselves. In dividing up property after a death, anxiety about money combined with grief so unsettles many families that they make lopsided decisions.

Sometimes the anxiety can slide into panic that reaches epic proportions. A man overhears a chance remark that real-estate values are falling and impulsively wants to sell his house. A large telephone bill turns into a demand for a divorce. A loss in the stock market generates careless buying in order to recoup. Financial panics themselves are triggered by everybody losing rationality at once.

Money creates at least some anxiety in everyone, for several powerful reasons. Few of us ever feel we have enough money. The idea of not being able to pay our bills is scary. More important, money is connected with a host of deep yearnings—the desire for immortality, the quest for security, the wish to be loved, the drive for power, the need for self-esteem. Being confronted with these powerful feelings often triggers anxiety, and a host of emotions we would rather not feel—envy, greed, guilt, competitiveness.

Anxiety in general exists to warn us that we're in the presence of something potentially dangerous—and money is certainly that.

The Emotions Money Unmasks

Ellen, a fifty-three-year-old magazine editor, is sitting at her desk on a Saturday morning paying her bills, a chore she loathes. The only way she can make herself do it is to bribe herself: when she finishes she and a friend are going to lunch, complete with a bottle of wine, at an expensive restaurant. As Ellen opens the drawer filled with a jumble of unpaid bills, canceled checks, and old receipts, she fights back the urge to slam it shut. She takes out a fistful of bills at random and places them next to her checkbook. Having no idea what her current balance is, she fishes around for her latest bank statement and, miraculously, finds it. Opening it, her heart sinks: she thought she had at least $500 more than she does. She automatically assumes the bank is correct and that she's once again lost track.

Ellen starts to write checks. She discovers a bill she had forgotten about, a department-store charge account. Upset, she flips it aside but then begins to panic—what are the penalties for late payment? Writing a few more checks, she forges ahead and finds the rent bill, knowing this one has to be paid on time.

The ordeal continues for another half hour, as long as Ellen can stand it. By the end of that time, she's exhausted; she has subjected herself to endless recriminations about her incompetence, disorganization, and general inadequacy, as well as endless resolutions to do better, get help, improve.

She can't wait to get downtown for that glass of wine—maybe a double martini would be better. Over lunch she asks her friend if he knows of anybody who can help her manage her money. He winces. "No," he says. "The whole subject makes me sick. How about another bottle."

Julie, a thirty-two-year-old real-estate saleswoman, is also paying the monthly bills. She isn't panicked, but she is worried. Her husband, Ted, recently quit his job as a computer salesman because there was too much pressure and because he hated being nice to people he didn't much like. He hasn't decided what to do next.

Money itself is a problem. If Ted stays out of work for more than a few months their savings will be gone. But beyond that, Julie is worried because staying at home is making Ted depressed. Suddenly, she has an idea. If Ted took care of their two preschoolers that might take his mind off himself for a while, not to mention all the money they would save on the housekeeper.

Julie is astonished at Ted's reaction to her plan. "Oh, great," he says nastily. "You want to turn me into a house husband so you can be out selling your fancy houses. Ever since you took over the checkbook you've gotten to be a goddam accountant."

"I didn't take it over," Julie says defensively. "You asked me to do it because you hate it."

"Wrong," Ted snaps. "You said I was irresponsible with money, so I said fine, you handle it."

Julie glares at him. "I just stepped in and did the work as usual. Somebody around here has to take care of the money and somebody has to make it. Maybe you don't like what I do for a living, but right now it's paying the mortgage."

"Is that all you ever think about? Money? Don't you care about what's going on with me at all? You're not the woman I married, that's for sure. That business has really changed you."

Bitter and misunderstood, Julie doesn't know whether to throw something at Ted or to cry.

Charles, a thirty-four-year-old CPA, leaves home on a clear September morning at eight as usual. He's already completed his three-mile run, had his melon and coffee, said goodbye to his wife as she left for work, and handed over his two children to the babysitter. Driving to work, he thinks about the decision he has to make. After ten years in the business, he's making $150,000 a year. Today he'll have the chance to make that amount in just a few hours if everything goes according to plan and if he's willing to bend the law in what he's almost sure is a foolproof scheme. He thinks of himself as a risk-taker and hates to let an opportunity pass. But his wife, a lawyer, tells him he's crazy even to think about it. What do they need with more money anyway? As he drives, the song lyrics on the car radio can't tell him what to do.

All of these stories are about problems caused by the emotional meanings of money. For Ellen, who avoids dealing with money unless she absolutely has to, who sinks into a state of anxious depression whenever she thinks about it, money means dependency, which some part of her craves. On some level, Ellen can't fully accept herself as an independent woman; it's as if being able to go it alone violated some rule. Even though she has enough money it causes her great anxiety to deal with it, because dealing with it means she has to face the fact that she has no one but herself to depend on.

For Ted, money is self-esteem, worth. Because he isn't bringing it in, he feels worthless. Instead of acknowledging that, he accuses Julie—who's treating money more realistically—of his own concerns, an overemphasis on the importance of money. When he says, "Is that all you ever think about? Money?" he's really saying, "I wish I didn't care so much about money so that I could get out of this depression and think constructively about what I want to do and feel good about myself again."

As for Charles, money for him means power and self-esteem. He isn't getting enough of either right now, and he's tempted to try to solve this problem by getting more money—even taking a catastrophically self-destructive risk to do so. Unless he finds other ways to feel better about himself, Charles probably will find himself wanting more and more money, discovering that it does the trick less and less well. As his risk-taking increases, he'll probably begin to feel guilt, which will make him feel even less powerful.

The Root of Evil—and Good

Where do these links between money and emotion come from? Traditional psychoanalytic theory ties money to the anal phase of development: a preoccupation with money goes along with a fussy personality that's hung up on issues of control, caused by a developmental arrest in the period of toilet training. More recent thinking has emphasized the importance of other periods of development on attitudes about money. Our feelings about money evolve as we grow, and money becomes a dynamic issue in each developmental stage.

Preschoolchildren in the Oedipal period are often concerned with feelings of competition and aggression; if they're made overly aware of a parent's money at that age, they may associate it with feelings of power and strength. School-age children are forming their ego-ideal, discovering what sort of person they want to be like. Family attitudes toward money may have an effect, and later in their lives money may become too closely connected with feelings of self-esteem. Children of that age are also beginning to tackle the reality of money as they negotiate an allowance, deal with a friend who has more money or possessions, or wrestle with the temptation to steal.

By adolescence, when the main tasks of development involve establishing an autonomous identity separate from, but still connected to, the family, money can come to mean freedom as well as dependence. Throughout each phase of development, money contributes to the shaping of key personal characteristics, such as self-image and self-esteem, moral values, political views, family role, general ambition and goals, and styles of dealing with people. Some children are naturally generous; others hoard. Some children grow up feeling rich; others with the same financial background feel poor. Some children hardly think about money, while others are budding tycoons with their roadside stands and car wash concessions.

Parents often underestimate the importance of what they teach their children about money and, more important, what they demonstrate by their actions. The whole idea of a "spoiled" child has more to do with underlying values and styles around money and material objects than it does with absolute amounts. A relatively poor child can be spoiled if he's sent the message that he's entitled to have everything; a rich child can learn honesty and social obligation through the handling of money.

When parents don't pay attention to the psychological importance of money they can make mistakes of lasting impact. Common mistakes include:

—Substituting money for love. That can leave a child with an enduring sense of resentment that no amount of money can cure.
—Being chronically inconsistent with money, which can create a deep insecurity around it.
—Habitually connecting money with personal worth, which can lead to overemphasizing the importance of money.
—Overindulging a child, which can lead to a sense of entitlement the real world can't gratify.
—Always withholding money in order to "build character." Unfortunately, the sort of character this builds is pretty gloomy.
—Never teaching children anything about money or giving them opportunities to handle it. Early ignorance can lead to almost phobic avoidance and helplessness later on.
—Overburdening children with financial worries without providing perspective or reassurance. This can lead to a host of problems, not the least of which is simply a terrifying atmosphere in which to grow up.

The developmental process proceeds throughout adulthood, and feelings connected with money may continue to change. But much of the unconscious or gut-level reactions to money have been established by early adulthood.

So for all of us at one time or another, money comes to mean something else. Money can be an antidepressant ("When the going gets tough, the tough go shopping"); it can be a substitute for love. Some people become addicted to making money to raise their self-esteem or because they need security. To some degree, money has all of these meanings for all of us. The problems occur when the meaning becomes overly weighted in a particular direction so that the *real* meaning of money—a tool to help us live our lives in comfort—becomes buried.

This kind of substitution thinking happens all the time without our noticing it. You feel unloved, so you ask for a raise. You feel insecure, so you increase the insurance on your house. Your self-esteem wanes, so you buy a snazzy sports car. The financial solution often fails, however, because the root problem was not financial. If you're feeling unloved the raise, even if you get it, won't take care of it. The additional insurance will only add to your worries; the car will give you a boost only for a week or a month.

Yet because spending money is easier than dealing with complex emotional problems, we often try the money cure first. A major aim of this book is to help you check that impulse, to stop you from wasting money by trying to make it solve emotional problems.

Two

Money as Love
and Self-Esteem

Most of us use money to express love or, at times, to withhold it. For most of us, our self-esteem is to some extent bound up with how much money we have. For some of us, though, money is the true scorecard, the real answer to the question, "What are you worth?"

How would you answer the following questions?

When you were a child, did you receive presents when what you wanted was affection or attention?

Were you encouraged to marry for money?

Did your parents show more affection to relatives who were rich?

Did (Do) you feel that if you made a lot of money you would have a different group of friends?

Do you feel that your spouse would stop loving you if you lost most of your money? Or that you would stop loving your spouse if he or she lost most of his or her money?

Do you manage to let people know how much you're worth or how much some expensive possession cost?

Do you live beyond your means?

Do you ever feel ashamed because you have less money than someone else?

Do you look down on people who work hard but make very little money?

If you answered "yes" to many of these questions, you may unconsciously equate money with love or self-esteem.

To some extent money is a perfectly rational means of expressing love. Many people use money to give pleasure to others, and to themselves as well, because there's pleasure in giving—altruism has its personal rewards. What is destructive is using money as a substitute for love or caring.

Alan, a divorced father, sends his two sons lavish presents but hardly ever sees them. He can't understand why they don't like him. "I give them everything under the sun. What more do they want?"

The man or woman who unconsciously equates love with money is often the product of a family in which there was money, but little affection. He grows up on a diet of money/no love and keeps the tradition alive. Because he never learned how to develop sustaining relationships with people, he relies on his relationship with money to sustain him. A person who equates money with love may feel that he literally can buy the love of a spouse or a child.

The song says, "Can't buy me love," yet people keep trying to do just that.

When All Else Fails, Try Money

Sarah was the oldest child of a wealthy insurance executive in Hartford, Connecticut. Educated at the best schools, she received the message from an early age that she was of the upper crust and that her goal should always be to be "the best," whatever that meant at the time. In grade school that meant the prettiest; in prep school it meant the smartest and the prettiest; in college it meant the smartest, the prettiest, and the most radical.

What Sarah never complained about, almost as if she didn't know what she was missing, was not receiving enough love. She took it in stride, as if it were the way of the world, that she seldom received praise or reassurance from her parents and that she always felt only as good as her last achievement. The many presents and the large allowance her parents gave her never seemed quite to make up for the affection and praise she wasn't getting.

A baby-boomer, Sarah attended college in the sixties; debutante was out, SDS was in. Mother, who drank to hide her depression, simultaneously urged her daughter to achieve and criticized her for it. At the root of her mother's ambivalence was, on the one hand, a desire for Sarah to achieve so that it would reflect well on her and, on the other hand, jealousy of Sarah's success and a desire for her to fail.

Father wondered what had happened to his little girl, but attributed her radical politics to adolescent rebellion. A star in the Radcliffe radical movement of the period, Sarah was hurt and outraged by her parents' lack of understanding; she attributed it to the inevitable outcome of a bourgeois lifestyle. She found a new family in the New Left and became an effective and visible spokesperson.

After graduation with high honors in political science Sarah moved to New York, where she worked tirelessly for a liberal newspaper. A New Age was upon us, and Sarah was in the vanguard.

As the romanticism and hope of the sixties gave way to the cynicism and pragmatism of the seventies, Sarah found herself taking pre-med courses. Medical school represented a last-ditch effort to combine her fading idealism with a practical way of making a living.

Maintaining independence from her family, Sarah made it through medical school on loans. After internship she became a general practitioner in rural Maine. At that point she began to give out. Her patients demanded far more of her than she had ever thought possible, and the intangible rewards she had hoped for seemed insufficient.

Sarah began a relationship with one of her friends from Harvard who lived in the area and who was making a lot of money in real-estate development. Within a year she had left medicine to join her friend in business. She became as zealous—and as effective—in her ability to make money as she had been in her ability to deal with politics.

She now became cynical, turning on her old friends and her old self with pitiless scorn. "We didn't mean a word of it," she would say. "We were just spoiled brats."

Over time Sarah became rich. She married her partner and had children whom she apportioned to the best schools and camps. But her cynicism became boundless. Even her husband, no Pollyanna himself, grew wary of her barbed remarks. She loved money. "It's the only thing you can trust." By the time Sarah was in her forties, she was isolated and rich, living out her life in a kind of holding action, waiting for it to end.

Sarah came to money as the court of last resort. What had always been missing from her life was love. As a child, she tried to get it by "being good." When that failed she tried to find it in the great group effort of politics in the sixties. When that failed she tried to get it as a doctor from her patients. Finally, after that enormous effort failed, she bitterly turned to money for love. She brought to bear all her determination and intelligence to get money and, of course, she succeeded. And, of course, she failed.

Sarah asked money to supply her with love, among other things in her life. There was nothing inherently wrong in anything Sarah did, from being a good student to political leader, to doctor, to entrepreneur. Indeed, in many ways, they were all highly commendable. Her unhappiness stemmed not from her actions but from her motivation— her *agreement,* to use our term. Finally, money came to represent salvation, which is, of course, an agreement money can't fulfill.

Many people like Sarah suffer early in their lives from defects in self-esteem because they don't feel praised, loved, or valued by the people around them, particularly their parents. The toddler's love affair with the world, rather than blossoming into a sustaining sense of confidence and self-worth, retreats into insecurity, skittishness, and self-doubt.

In adulthood such people seek to repair this kind of early injury in a number of ways, some adaptive, such as doing good for others, some frustratingly maladaptive, such as abusing drugs or pursuing fame for its own sake.

Sarah found that the more altruistic remedies didn't work, so she turned to money as her cure. When the pursuit of money becomes the pursuit of love, it usually fails because it sidesteps the underlying feeling of worthlessness. If the early injury to self-esteem came from being poor, money might heal it. But if it came from neglect, inattention, or ridicule, money has very little curative power.

As you will see from the chapters that follow, people appeal to money to fill a number of emotional needs. As hard as it is to get money, common to all of us is the feeling that it's easier to get money than to fulfill the real, underlying need. Nowhere is this more evident than when one seeks money as a substitute for love.

Money as Self-Esteem: You Are What You Make?

Not many of us have enough of the kind of self-esteem that comes from within, a sense of our basic worth derived from sustaining experiences in childhood. People high in this kind of self-esteem value money and want to be paid fairly for what they do, but they don't rely on money to make them like themselves.

Far more common are people whose level of self-esteem is average or low. In our society, with the high value it places on financial "worth," money seems one of the best ways of raising it. In part because of that, many people find it hard to maintain a rational balance between their money and their self-esteem. Even though they know better, they get down on themselves for not having enough money, or high on themselves for having so much of it. Money can become the sole external meter of one's worth as a person, the stand-in for more constructive sources of self-esteem.

How does Sam, who won an award as the best high school science teacher in the city, feel when he compares his salary to an investment banker's? The dollar value society places on what you've chosen to do with your life obviously influences the way you feel about yourself. Sarah's story demonstrates the inefficacy of money as a substitute for another source of self-esteem: loving one's work. Consider the physician who takes on too many patients, hoping that increased income will make up for decreased job satisfaction. Variations on that happen to many young adults today. When they embark on high-paying careers in areas they find less than satisfying, they underestimate the importance of liking what they do for a living. As their dissatisfaction grows they often change the type or structure of their work, but they count on money, preferably more of it, to make things magically fine.

Even someone with high self-esteem is affected to some extent by the amount of money he has or makes. It takes a lot of self-esteem to feel untouched by the difference between the way the maitre d' at the best restaurant in town treats you if you go once a year, and the way he treats the local millionaire who has a regular table. Money equated with self-esteem makes people do crazy things. A house that can't be sold for $250,000 sells instantly when the price goes up to

17

$350,000. The seller understands that people aren't purchasing houses, they're buying self-esteem. For $250,000 you get only a house, for $350,000 you get a new you.

One paradoxical effect of our culture's behavioral conditioning is that people actually *lose* self-esteem by going after the money they believe will raise it. Deep down, they may know they could feel better about themselves by, say, becoming involved in volunteer work rather than by working harder for more money, but they act the way society tells them to act.

Money as Self-Esteem: Less May Be More

The converse of money as self-esteem exists less often in our society, but sometimes people are subject to a reverse group ethic. Mark, a professor of anthropology, finds himself shunned by his colleagues when his documentary film about the punk-rock culture becomes a commercial success. Mark, who had felt proud of his achievement, is hurt to discover that making a lot of money from his work is considered crude by his friends. Certain groups—academia is one of them—whose members don't make much money prevent money from becoming too closely attached to self-esteem by attacking the self-esteem of those who do make money, especially if they make the money in a way that's connected with their work. (The connection may be too close for comfort. Why, his colleagues may be asking themselves, didn't they think of making that movie?)

In certain circumstances, the financial hairshirt becomes a badge of honor and money a scarlet letter. One research scientist who married a millionaire has a modest apartment near her institute and a grand house in the country to which she rarely invites her colleagues. The display of wealth, even if it didn't come from the work, is at best in bad taste.

Three

Money as Security and Freedom

Everyone equates money with security. What's odd is that many people with very little money feel secure, while others who have a lot of money feel quite the opposite. To start examining your own feelings about money as security, ask yourself the following questions.

When you were a child, did your parents fuss over nickels and dimes?

Was money a topic of such concern in your family that even as a small child you worried about financial disasters?

Were your parents so vague about money that you never knew where you or your family stood?

Did anyone in your family go broke or get into a disastrous situation because of money?

As an adult, do you think you worry unnecessarily about money?

Have you taken jobs for the financial security they offered?

Are you overinsured?

Have you lost much money by being overly cautious with your investments?

Do you believe we're headed for another Great Depression? Have you taken any action based on that belief?

If you got a substantial raise, would you still feel as insecure as you do now?

Is money the chief reason you aren't doing what you want to do now?

When you fantasize about having a lot of money, do you first think about how to protect it?

If you answered "yes" to many of these questions, then money, for you, equates with security and freedom.

Money as Security: How Much Is Enough?

No one is truly secure. We will all die someday; we might die at any moment, and so might those we love. We live with the knowledge that we may suddenly become permanently disabled, lose our livelihood, our home, our mind. In a less catastrophic vein, we deal with minor evidence of life's insecurity every day—will it rain for the picnic?

We combat our potentially overwhelming insecurity in various ways—belief in God, reliance on family, community structure, the law, daily routine, traffic and weather reports, and, of course, on our ability to get money.

It's not surprising that people look to money for security. As mere mortals, we can never be completely secure. We could all use more security, and most of us could use more money. But when money comes to *mean* security, we're in danger of being chronically dissatisfied. You will never have as much as you want of either.

When it comes to money, though, it ought to be possible, with luck and good planning, to have *enough*. To some extent, money does mean security—*financial* security.

Still, what does "financial security" mean? A TV commercial shows a man in a business suit running down a football field, with a team of insurance agents as his blockers, charging toward his goal of "financial security." How much will it take to create that? Some people who live on a small pension are financially secure, while others with millions are frantic.

Often financial insecurity has strong roots in real-life experiences. Many people who lived through the Depression of the 1930s, for instance, never get over the feeling that doomsday could arrive tomorrow, that you can never have enough. Growing up poor creates similar worries. And in some families, the sense of chronic, gnawing anxiety about money seems to be passed along with the genes.

Curiously, the same experience can have very different effects on people. Consider Rachel and Ann, sisters now in their fifties. Their parents owned a chain of Laundromats and did reasonably well. But like their business, which was literally nickel and dime, they fretted constantly about small amounts of money. The family motto was, "Watch out for the pennies and the dollars will take care of themselves," in part because several relatives had gone bankrupt. Although their parents were loving, the children were spanked if they ever lost any of their belongings. In their prayers every night, both girls asked to have enough money when they grew up.

As is so often the case, the two sisters' adult response to the same early situation was very different. Rachel devoted herself to making money. More than anything else, she wanted to get rid of the feeling of financial insecurity. She became a successful lawyer, learned her way around the stock market, and had her first million by the time she was forty. Despite that, she was still discontented: now she was tortured by fantasies about losing what she'd made. She had learned the lessons her parents taught her too well.

Ann, on the other hand, developed a cheerful disdain for money. After college she became a writer and supported herself by taking various odd jobs. For a year she was a letter carrier; after publishing her first book she got a job as an English teacher at a private school. She lived simply and never seemed to mind.

Rachel emerged from her childhood desperately wanting to make money; Ann grew up wanting to be done with the subject altogether. She deeply resented the stranglehold it had on her parents and the way it had influenced her upbringing. Her method of defeating it was simply to ignore the subject. Rachel tried to outmuscle money; Ann stepped out of the ring entirely. Oddly, Ann ended up feeling more financially secure than her wealthy sister.

"Why won't you take anything from me?" Rachel often asked Ann. "There aren't any strings attached and it would make me feel good."

"But it would make me feel bad," Ann would answer. "I'm not being proud. I just don't want to come near it. Maybe I'm like the child of alcoholics who won't take that first drink for fear of becoming one. I have enough money, and one way or another I know I always will. That's all I want."

Rachel and Ann demonstrate another odd fact about financial security. Those like Ann, who set out to make "enough," can often reach that goal. But those like Rachel, who set out to make "more," usually discover that more is never enough. Just as children of alcoholic or abusive parents often end up marrying a mate with the same problem in an unconscious attempt to make it come out better this time, so Rachel "married" her parents' attitude toward money in order to fix it. Although she accomplished her goal of making a lot of money, she failed in her attempt at emotional repair.

Of course, not all people who are overly insecure about money went through such childhood experiences. Leo is a financial planner who grew up in a family that had plenty of money. Bright and creative, he thought of going into business on his own. But he worried that he wouldn't get enough clients, so he took the more secure route of working for a large firm. Recently, he developed a personalized investment plan that he thinks could market very well, but his fear of losing the financial security his job gives him keeps him from taking the risk to get it off the ground.

The causes of this common kind of financial insecurity, which prevents a person from taking aggressive action, have to do with unresolved Oedipal conflicts. In Freudian terms, the child wants to possess the parent of the opposite sex but fears punishment from the other parent and so represses the wish. Resolution normally occurs in adolescence, as the child becomes independent. For some people, though, the fear of punishment persists so strongly that independent assertive action becomes impossible. The fear is not wholly conscious. Rather, it is a dim but powerful sensation of danger connected with standing up for oneself or being spontaneous, creative, or independent. It feels to such a person as if decisive action is dangerous or forbidden, and that with success will come an even greater loss, such as that of a parent's love or one's basic secure place in the world. Feelings of insecurity or danger around self-assertion can lead to a generalized holding back or fear of success. Making money (or not making money) is a common stage on which to act out this conflict.

Short of psychoanalysis, the best way around this problem is simply to make some changes, take some risks, and discover that it's not as dangerous as you thought. Be careful, though, because it's at these moments that people unconsciously sabotage their own efforts. The tennis player who can always get the lead but never win the game is one example. Or the man or woman who deserves a promotion but who always flubs it when making his or her case for it. For that reason, external support and guidance can be helpful. In any case, bear in mind that what you *perceive* as financial insecurity may not have much to do with money. Instead, that insecurity may be your unconscious way of holding yourself back, keeping yourself in your place, under your

father's or your boss's or society's thumb. Financial insecurity may simply be your rationalization for not acting
more boldly. Because the unconscious fear is very powerful,
it can actually prevent you from striving for the success you
consciously desire.

If you're unreasonably insecure about money, try setting
an actual figure that would be enough, rather than simply
trying to get more. The initial step in coming to terms with a
tendency to treat money as security is to separate the idea of
having enough money—financial security—from the larger
human need for security itself. The first is attainable; the
second, unfortunately, is not. If you load money with all your
yearnings for security, you will join that large group of
people who can never have enough money.

Money as Freedom: "The Someday Syndrome"

If everyone equates money with security, almost everyone
equates money with freedom. What keeps you from doing
what you want to do all day? Money probably ranks near the
top of the list. Pursuing money to gain freedom makes
perfect sense. Problems arise when we use money as a reason
for *not* seeking freedom.

How much money would it take to make you feel free to do
what you want with your life? The almost universal answer
is, "More than I have," although sometimes even the very
rich can feel trapped, rather than freed, by their money and
the necessity of caring for it. The amount of money we need
to buy the exhilarating feeling of freedom becomes a fleet-
ing figure, a money mirage, always receding on the horizon
even as we pursue it. "I could do whatever I wanted if I had

$50,000 a year," you say when you're twenty-five. At thirty-five the figure is up to $100,000, and at forty-five it may be much higher again.

The problem is both real and illusory. Unfortunately, expenses normally rise along with earning power. We generally do need more money as we grow older. But the psychological illusion lies in our refusal to see that most of us are, in fact, free all the time, that we choose to trap ourselves.

To accept that idea is extremely difficult if you're not happy with your life. "I'm where I am because I chose to be here," is hard to say without feeling bad. So we look for something to blame, and money is a prime candidate. "If only I had enough money I would change my life." As frustrating as it is to say that, it may feel better than saying, "I don't have the guts to change my life."

How much of your enslavement to money is real? Could it be that you're blaming money when what's holding you back is lack of nerve? It's far better not to become trapped in what we call the Someday Syndrome:

"Someday I'll sail around the world." "Someday I'll start my own business." "Someday I'll go back to painting." "Someday I'll clear enough time to write a book." "Someday I'll spend the summer camping with the kids." "Someday I'll get my broker's license." "Someday I'll . . ."

The sad fact is that for almost every Someday Syndromer, someday never comes. And as time passes the dream fades, losing its vibrancy, until it's only a memory evoked by certain songs.

The best way to manage the Someday Syndrome is simply to recognize it. Test the reality of your financial needs against what you imagine them to be. Ask yourself if you're using "not enough money" as an excuse for not doing what you really want to do. Like work that expands to fill the time allotted for it, financial needs expand to drain all the money

25

available to fill them. For a host of emotional reasons, people avoid using money in ways that would make them most happy, and then blame their unhappiness on money.

The Chains Money Makes: The Freedom of the Ascetic

Occasionally you come across a person who avoids money almost entirely. Happy with his poverty, suspicious of the material world, the ascetic actively resists having money. He tries to simplify his life, to free himself of as many financial obligations as possible. Not unlike the man or woman who vows chastity, the ascetic vows poverty to prevent money from leading him astray.

The true ascetic is as disciplined about money as the most committed entrepreneur. As the entrepreneur tries to find ever more clever ways to make money, so the ascetic puts his mind to avoiding money's temptations. It's hard to say which takes more work: getting rich or living poor. It's fair to say that both extremes tax one's ingenuity.

Unlike most poverty, voluntary poverty is not caustic to the spirit. True ascetics are convincing about what amounts to the ecstasy of their way of life. There are many different sources of asceticism, but the common pathway has to do with spiritual need. Most extreme remedies, such as asceticism, derive from extreme needs. The ability to comply with an extreme remedy requires great strength.

It would trivialize the ascetic's experience to dismiss it as masochism, or an expression of unconscious guilt, or a response to a fear of one's own greed. It is most often a highly disciplined and creative attempt to deepen one's spiritual life by avoiding the distractions of the material world. Asceticism has held a place in the American grain at least since Thoreau and provides a cautionary counterpoint to the conspicuous consumption we usually associate with our society.

Of a far different stripe is the person who is forever insisting money doesn't matter, but who secretly craves it. He affects an air of moral superiority, of being "above" the money-hungry rest of us; in private he eats his heart out with envy and greed. His insistent lack of interest in money is what gives him away.

His agreement with money is one of reverse psychology or downright hypocrisy. If I pretend not to care, he thinks, maybe people will trust me enough so that I can take advantage of them. If I treat money with disdain, perhaps money will court me.

Alternatively, money for this sort of pseudo-ascetic may be a forbidden fruit. His desire for it is so wrapped up in guilt and shame that he has to pretend he doesn't want it at all. He is so ashamed of the part of him that wants money that he hides it, showing people only a disdain for money, the attitude that it doesn't matter.

Money as Guilt

The shame and guilt surrounding money is not confined to the pseudo-ascetic. At one time or another, most of us have had to deal with guilt in our handling of money.

We know that money is powerful—often more powerful even than sex. The average person would not uproot his family and move across the country for sex, but he almost certainly would for enough money.

Money is often associated with greed and corruption. "Filthy rich" is a phrase that still lives in our language; money often implies the "dirtier," less pure aspects of human nature. The amateur athlete, for instance, plays for the fun of it; the professional for the money. It's as if the transition from amateur to professional, from no money to money, involves a loss of innocence. A phrase like, "Never mix business with pleasure," translates easily to, "Never mix money with friendship." Most striking of all is what we call getting a lot of money all at once—"making a killing." Enormous profit metaphorically equates with murder.

This meaning of money frequently leads to self-destructive behavior. Some people feel too guilty to hold onto money, believing that the advantage gained by having money is in some way unfair. Money is a symbol of greed, privilege, corruption—badness in general. Having money makes such a person feel guilty. In order to relieve the guilt, he or she gets rid of the money, often in foolish, self-defeating ways.

It's the meaning of money that's confused here. Rather than seeing money as a tool that can be used to good purpose, such a person perceives money as inextricably entwined with evil forces. Instead of undoing the tangle, he tries to stay away from money altogether.

Consider Gail, the forty-year-old curator of a metropolitan museum. She consulted a psychiatrist for help with handling money, and she told the following story. "You won't believe this, but four years ago I was a rich woman, and now I'm almost broke. Four years ago my mother died and left me a large sum of money. My job at the museum doesn't pay much, and I felt overjoyed to have the nest egg.

"Or so I thought. Actually, I hated it. I didn't know what to do with it. I began giving it away, even to causes I knew hardly anything about. Each time I'd give some away I'd feel good for a while, and then I'd start obsessing about the money again, wondering what right I had to so much money. I hadn't earned it, and I just didn't feel as if I deserved it. So I kept getting rid of it."

In psychotherapy, Gail worked on separating her feelings of low self-esteem relating to competition with her mother from the money itself. She began to see that her guilt, although a real feeling, was irrational; she had done nothing wrong. Unfortunately, she had lost a lot of money before reaching the point where she could allow herself to have any.

Central to a problem like Gail's is a clash between what you are and what you think you ought to be. How can I have money and still be a good person? How can I be like all those rich people and still stand up for what is real and true in life?

In fact, having money often does corrupt, but it isn't really the money that's corrupting. Rather, it's that part of you that uses money in a corrupt way. If this point can be kept clear, and if you are capable of acting in a way that is consonant with your own values, money can enable rather than corrupt.

It is a strikingly counterintuitive fact that honesty and integrity around money is not proportional to the amount of money you have. Many poor people are meticulously honest with their money and many rich people chronically cheat on their taxes. The internal permission one grants oneself to break the law is related more to one's sense of personal entitlement and greed than to financial need.

Four

Money as Power and Independence

We all believe, to some degree, that money provides power and independence. The following questions address the nature of this connection.

Did your father control your mother through money, or vice versa?

Have you frequently fired people who work for you?

Do you feel that the best method for getting your own way is to have the most money?

Do your fantasies of having a lot of money include scenes like taking revenge on people who have hurt you, controlling the people around you, or changing social or political policy?

Do you believe that the most powerful people in the world are rich?

When you get into arguments with your spouse, is money the usual topic?

If, for you, the meaning of money is weighted toward power and control, you probably answered "yes" to many of these questions.

The Impotence of Power

Roger is a very rich man. He grew up in an affluent family with a long tradition of philanthropy, particularly in the arts, and he spent his college years at Princeton as a good-natured and well-liked fellow. Beneath that facade, though, Roger struggled with recurring episodes of depression. The more his friends told him what a good guy he was, the more he heard them saying he was nothing special. He tagged himself with a phrase his grandmother used to dismiss people with no particular talent: "not much of a much."

After college, unable to find a place for himself in any of the "creative" fields, Roger turned to business with an almost bitter determination. On entering business school, his conscious agreement with money was clear: I will show them all by becoming very, very rich. He turned down the financial assistance his family offered and began, at age twenty-two, to live the myth of the self-made man. His spontaneous affability changed to controlled and polished charm. He drew on his upbringing and education to develop skills of subtle intimidation. By the time he was in his late twenties, the good-guy undergraduate had become a shrewd master of the real-estate business. Roger secretly delighted in the effect of his presence at meetings. With each passing year he could dismiss ever more influential figures as being "not much of a much."

Having amassed a large fortune by age thirty-five, Roger turned his sights on the field he felt most rejected by: the arts. Those "creative" people who had treated him with condescension would have to bow to him now. He bought a leading publishing house and let everyone there know he expected more originality from the people in charge. His net impact was to replace one editorial staff with another, almost identical staff.

31

Now forty and a well-known patron of the arts, Roger attended the symphony one evening. He surveyed the audience as the music played and felt chords of self-congratulation swell within him. During intermission he was delighted to overhear two women of obvious breeding talking about him, about a rumor that he might be persuaded to become a patron of music, having "done" literature. "But," one of the women said, "he's such an unhappy fellow. Could we bear to have him around?"

Everyone in the room, even the room itself, might as well have disappeared. It wasn't only what the woman had said but her tone of voice, so like his grandmother's, that plummeted him back into the depression of his college years.

For a few weeks he let down his guard and spoke openly about the emptiness of his life, his vacuous marriage, his lack of friends, his remorse at having used money as an instrument of vengeance, because vengeance was now being visited on him.

The moment of insight, however, was too painful for him to hold onto. Soon he "came to his senses," ascribed his depression to overwork and a virus he picked up from his wife, and returned to work with a newfound interest in music.

Roger's agreement with money, deliberately made and expertly executed, worked exactly as he had planned. He was able, through money, to give himself what he once felt he lacked: power, specialness, muchness. But money couldn't repair that fundamental sense of inadequacy summed up by his grandmother's dismissal. Until he came to terms with that, he would continue to use money, not as a tool of love in the philanthropic tradition of his family, but as a tool of hate.

The tendency to be deceived by money isn't curbed by intelligence. Roger was an exceedingly bright man, although he could never really give himself credit for that. He used his intelligence to get him what he thought he wanted, only to discover it wasn't enough. By then, however, he was committed to a course he couldn't veer from.

Money as Power and Control: "Every Man Has His Price"

The power of money can do good, even great good. Few of us would work without a salary. Properly placed financial incentives can get the best out of people. The power of money steers medical research and fuels the arts. But without question, money also controls people in destructive ways. Money is the power a man uses to get a woman into bed when she doesn't want to be there, or to keep a wife in a bad marriage. Money is the power parents have to make a child attend a particular college or enter a certain profession, the power an employer has to make an employee do something he doesn't want to or shouldn't do.

The examples of money as a negative controlling influence are rampant. One of our greatest sources of control over our children is economic. A child is dependent for virtually every purchase he makes on his parents' money, not to mention his very food and shelter.

Parents can use this power wisely or they can be destructive with it. Hal, the forty-seven-year-old owner of a hardware store, tells a familiar story. "Why am I working here? Do you think I care about paint and nails? My father always wanted me to take over his business. I wanted to run a restaurant, and I did for a while. When the restaurant failed and I was deep in debt with a family to support, my father said he'd bail me out if I'd take over the store. I tried not to, but there was no other way. I was trapped. One year led to another. Now he says if I sell it he'll cut the whole family out of his will and give it all to charity. How can I do that to my kids? So I'm stuck."

Hal's father dominated his son through money. If a child grows up in a similar atmosphere, he's likely to repeat the pattern as an adult. Either he will fear the power of money and be unduly intimidated by it, or he will crave money and use it himself in a bullying way.

Although we accept as normal the economic power of parents over children (so long as it isn't abused), the economic power battles between men and women are a different matter.

Consider Martha and Peter, now in their early forties, with two teenage children. Martha gave up her job as a copywriter when they married, and she has stayed at home ever since. Peter's career in advertising has recently skyrocketed. He travels a great deal and has let Martha know he's met a lot of people who make her seem boring and stupid.

Although he denies it, Martha is convinced that Peter is having affairs. She doesn't really want a divorce. She worries about what that would do to the kids, and she still loves Peter. Once he calms down from his success, she believes, he will love her again. Nevertheless, after one particularly bitter quarrel, she broaches the subject of divorce.

"If you do that," Peter responds, "I'll make sure you get next to nothing. There are ways to do that. I can quit work for one thing. I can cut you down so you're living in a walk-up worrying about the electric bill. Do you think I've achieved all of this, on my own I might add, just to pay you?"

Not surprisingly, Martha feels trapped by Peter's use of money as control.

Americans have traditionally entertained ambivalent feelings about money as a source of power. We both despise and admire Alexis, the character Joan Collins plays on *Dynasty*, who isn't afraid to use money to control others' lives. We get a kick out of *Dallas*'s J. R. Ewing, who acts out our fantasy about how wicked we would be, given enough money. And we warm to the stories of real-life tycoons like the Rocke-fellers and Trumps.

But we also identify with the little guy who gets pushed around by money. We thrill to the story in which money is defied and the fat cat loses.

Somewhere between those extremes we monitor our own power game with money. If you use money a great deal to push people around, you might consider whom you're really battling. And if you feel excessively controlled by money, you might consider whether some of that control is illusory. As with those who suffer from the Someday Syndrome, you may be blaming money for your own inability to take action.

Money as Independence: Having No Other Needs

Just as money can come to symbolize power and control, it also can be used to symbolize independence or, conversely, dependency.

We are all dependent to some degree, and each of us deals with those feelings differently. Some people are frightened by the feeling and try to behave as if they weren't dependent at all. The person who hates getting presents, who always picks up the check, who reflexively rejects the cup of coffee or the better chair or a hand with some work probably is made extremely uncomfortable by feelings of dependency. He may feel that his needs are too great or in some way unacceptable, so he denies that he has needs at all. People who feel this way often choose careers like medicine, in which others are dependent on them. Their discomfort with dependency may have originated with a family attitude that stressed self-reliance and scorned that part of the child that sought to be dependent. In some way, the child received the message to pretend he had no needs.

The problem is that those needs don't just disappear. They surface somewhere, often in dependence on things, not people: food, alcohol, drugs, tobacco, and, of course, money. Such a person may develop an almost addictive relationship with money; he needs his daily fix. Cheerfully going about his business, taking care of everybody else's needs, he is silently, unconsciously developing an over-reliance on money to take care of him, at the expense of reciprocal human relationships.

Money as Action: Catching the Fever

In Chapter 1, we discussed the anxiety money creates in all of us. For most people, that anxiety is an unpleasant feeling. For some, however, typically those for whom money means independence and power, what begins as anxiety becomes a thrill. The gambling term "action" is the appropriate definition of money for such people. While some pursue action by going after power and others by getting involved in exciting love affairs or dangerous sports, these people go after action through money.

Such a person can flee the interdependence of human relationships through action. He can feel relatively independent of the daily demands of spouse, family, and friends by developing a whirlwind relationship with money. That is where his heart lies; the others have to watch—cheering or fretting.

Action isn't for the fainthearted. Some would say it isn't for anyone with any sense, or that, like any drug, money as action dissolves values and morality by making victory the only concern. But there's a good argument for the other side: people who cannot only take competition but who thrive on it, who seek pressure and grow from it, who enjoy confrontation and uncertainty, are the men and women who make this country great.

The moral debate aside, let's simply point out that money does take on a very heady meaning for some people. When it reaches the stage of meaning action, it has gone beyond the normal anxiety/excitement we all feel around money and has become a potentially addictive euphoric substance.

Will started psychotherapy when he was forty-two, "to dry out," as he put it, though he wasn't hooked on alcohol. "I need a fix all the time. Nothing can match what it feels like to spot a deal and land it. It's like I've got this furnace inside me."

Over time, Will began to revive his interest in people and used therapy to explore parts of his past and himself he had used action to avoid. By the end, he remained an active financier, but he and his wife felt he had reclaimed his old self.

Of money's many meanings, money as action is the most immediately toxic, the most like a drug. Will was able to regain control of his life, kicking the self-defeating aspects of money as action. Most people have a lot more difficulty in doing so. Often a major crisis—divorce or bankruptcy or being caught breaking the law—has to occur before the person will seek outside help. As Will pointed out, the action is so much fun, such a high, that most people, once hooked, aren't motivated to change.

Of course, as dangerous as it can be, money as action can also be exciting and productive. Many rich and happy people are "psyched" by money, and their lives are energized by its pursuit. The point is to be in charge of the action, rather than letting the action control you.

Money as Dependency: Holding On

At the other end of the spectrum are people who fear independence. They are always seeking support, asking for directions, representing themselves as less competent or knowledgeable than they really are, always creating situations in which they have to be taken care of.

For people like that, money can symbolize the terrifying prospect of being on their own. They tend to give someone else responsibility for their finances. Sometimes they try to induce others to take care of them totally, providing both the management of the money and the money itself. Having or handling money comes to represent something frightening: a state of not being taken care of, a state of independence. As the person who fears dependence may rely on money too heavily, the person who fears independence may unconsciously sabotage his finances repeatedly.

Consider Becky, a sixty-year-old woman whose husband left her half a million dollars. Consciously, she knew that if she invested the money wisely it could support her for the rest of her life. Unconsciously, she feared the independence and loneliness it represented. Through a series of financial bungles, she managed over a period of five years to reduce her capital to $70,000. Now her children have to help her out. She achieved her unconscious goal of remaining dependent.

One of the easiest places to see how money becomes equated with dependency (or independence) is in adolescence, a struggle characterized by ambivalence. The parents are saying, "Please grow up! Please don't grow up!" The child is saying, "Please let me grow up and be on my own! Please let me stay a kid!"

These battles are often waged with the weapon of money. Parents who don't want their child to grow up (and every parent feels that way some of the time) can subtly maintain a child's dependency through money. They can do it by withholding money or, more deftly, by providing too much. Who prefers mowing lawns to a summer in Europe? Similarly, the child who doesn't want to grow up can maintain an economic dependence on his or her parents that will ensure a lasting, if not altogether pleasant bond.

On the other hand, a teenager who wants independence may go to great lengths to ensure it, by refusing his parents' money for tuition at a private college and working his way through a state university instead. A typical battle might go like this:

PARENT: Now let me get this straight. You want me to give you a hundred dollars a month for expenses, but you don't want me to ask where the money goes.

CHILD: Yes. Just stay off my back.

PARENT: But it's my money.

CHILD: And it's my life. I told you I could earn the money myself if I could work at T.C.'s, but you don't want me to.

PARENT: I don't like that crowd down there. You could work somewhere else. You know there's a lot of drugs at T.C.'s.

CHILD: So you automatically think I'll take them. Okay, so pay me yourself.

PARENT: All right. Give T.C.'s a try.

CHILD: Oh, great. You're saying, "Go ahead, son, become a drug addict. It's more important for me to keep my precious hundred bucks a month."

A key to resolving these situations is to realize that the battle isn't about money, but about dependence and independence, separation, growing up, letting go, all components of the relationship between a parent and a child.

Money as dependency shows up at many stages of life. A person stays in a low-paying job because the next step up would make employees dependent on him. A woman relinquishes all financial control to her husband so that she can preserve a dependent position. In order to avoid these traps, you need to examine your feelings of dependence and independence and how money bolsters or reduces those feelings. The goal is to learn to depend on money for what money can do, not to be enticed into some other arrangement.

Five

The Meaning of
Money for Couples

Marriages these days may be made or broken at the bank more often than in the bedroom. Frequently, arguments about money are really about something else, but money is a safer subject to fight about:

—A fight erupts about how much it costs to visit the in-laws. What they're really fighting about is his feelings about her parents.
—A fight erupts about the telephone bill. What's really at issue is his jealousy of the time she spends talking to her friends instead of to him.
—She nags him constantly to make more money. The real issue is her inability to come to terms with other lacks she sees in him.
—They can't manage money, and every month they fight about who's responsible for the chaos. What's really at issue is that each of them secretly wants to be taken care of.

Conversely, there are times when the real issue is money, but a couple prefers to camouflage it rather than talk about it:

—He hates what he does for a living and resents her for not working. So he nags her repeatedly about her housekeeping.

—She really wants him to make more money. Instead of telling him that, she attacks what he does in his spare time.

—They both work and earn a lot, but they're both bad with money. They talk about how hard it is to deal with the stress in their lives, but they never tackle the subject of financial planning.

—They're thinking about getting married, but each of them is worried about the other's earning power. Instead of talking about that, they begin to find fault with other aspects of their relationship.

It would be nice if there were a simple solution to the problems money causes between men and women. About the simplest that exists, though, isn't easy: learn to talk with your partner about money and what money means.

Part of that involves taking some history—your own and your partner's. If you'll think back to David and Franny in the Introduction, who argued about which house to buy, their fight escalated because neither one was aware of what money meant to the other. If you know your husband incurred a gambling debt in college from which he's never recovered emotionally, you may find it easier to deal with his miserliness. If you know your wife's drive to make top dollar comes from her father's telling her she'd never make "real money," you may be less likely to resent her single-mindedness.

If you can bring yourself to discuss money with your partner, if you can make yourself discover its meanings to you as individuals, and as a couple with shared goals, you may be able to keep money from becoming a negative factor. Some subjects to open up:

—How does each of you feel about who earns the money? Does either of you feel entitled to rewards because of the money earned? Is there unspoken resentment?

—Who controls the money? If the control isn't equal, is that a negotiated arrangement or one that "just happened"? If it just happened, is it perpetuating a situation of dependency or control?

—Who wants what from money? Are your visions for the future similar? It's amazing how couples can work at cross-purposes simply by never leveling with each other. "What do you mean you never wanted this house by the lake? I've been slaving for years to buy it for you." "What do you mean you would rather have had me at home more? You always told me we needed the money." Ideally, the sacrifices as well as the rewards of building a life together should be borne equally, which is a lot likelier to happen if money is talked about.

For Richer or for Poorer: Accounting for Romance

Discussing feelings about money is particularly important when marriage is in the air. Because money is the clearest ticket to independence we have, it's often the last thing talked about honestly when we enter into the dependent setup of a couple. Taking a good look at how you and your potential spouse deal with money can only help assure a smoother future. Without that, you will misunderstand each other at best, and run the risk of tyrannizing or torturing each other.

Trouble often develops when the wife-to-be makes more than her fiancé. Some women in this position complain that many men are turned off and feel intimidated. Other women acknowledge a difficulty in getting past their own expectations that the man should earn more.

Laura, a thirty-five-year-old lawyer, makes $130,000 a year, six times what Justin, a private school teacher, makes. "What can I do?" Laura says. "I want a family and kids, but I don't want to marry the kind of fast-track men I work with. And most other men I meet are threatened by me because I'm successful. Justin's one of the few exceptions, but I have my own problems with the idea of being married to someone who makes a fraction of what I do."

Laura, like many women and men, equates money with power, and, like many women, Laura wants a powerful man. If she can separate money from power, she may find other sources of power in Justin. If she can't, she may have let a good one get away.

Getting these issues into the open is difficult because it involves exposing parts of ourselves we prefer to keep hidden, such as the desire to dominate, or the wish to be loved more, or bad habits or bad luck. But in the open is the only place those issues can be dealt with and perhaps overcome.

Six

Your Agreement
with Money

We need to understand the dynamics of our relationship with money, a relationship fused with energy, unpredictability, and emotion. If we don't, we risk, as we do in human relationships, falling into repetitive, self-defeating patterns.

At the heart of everyone's relationship with money is an agreement, either spoken or silent, that governs our daily behavior. You can define your agreement with money by answering two questions:

1. What do I want from money?
2. What am I willing, and unwilling, to do to get money?

The first question asks what money means to you and what you expect from it. Depending on the extent to which this book has so far helped you to understand your feelings about money, your answers may range from certain material objects, to freedom and security, to self-esteem and sex appeal. Your objectives may be reasonable and attainable, or wildly irrational and impossible. In answering the first question as honestly as you can, you can begin to determine whether your agreement with money makes sense.

The second question turns the tables, giving money a chance to respond: "Okay, if you want me so much, what are you willing to do to have me?" The question should serve to reacquaint you with or remind you of the critical decisions you've always made about earning money. There are some activities no amount of money could make worthwhile, just as there are some offers almost no one can refuse.

No matter how honest you are with yourself, though, some part of your agreement with money lies buried. In this respect, your agreement is similar to those of other relationships, such as your agreement with your spouse. The explicit and conscious part of that agreement may be, "If I do the dishes on Monday, Wednesday, and Friday you will do them on Tuesday, Thursday, and Saturday; on Sunday we'll flip a coin." The implicit or unconscious part of that agreement may be, "If I do the dishes on Monday, Wednesday, and Friday you will think of me as the perfect husband, uncommonly magnanimous, irresistibly fair, and you will treat me as if I were God." Another spouse's conscious agreement might be, "If I postpone going back to school so we can have a baby, then you will cut back at work to help with the baby after it's born." The unconscious part of the agreement may be, "If I postpone going back to school so I can have a baby, you will do everything I want you to for the next ten years and you will treat me like a queen."

Sometimes agreements involve people and money at the same time. Your explicit agreement with your boss, for example, might be, "If you pay me $30,000 a year I'll do the work you ask of me every working day all year." The unconscious agreement may be, "If I work hard you will make me feel good about myself and give me all the approval and respect my father denied me."

Determining your agreement with money itself is tricky. You may say, "My agreement with money is simple. I expect it to pay my bills and give me a general sense of security. In return, I'll work hard to make money." Behind that conscious agreement, though, there may be an unconscious agreement that goes like this: "I expect money to make me feel powerful, sexy, and lovable. I expect money to be there when I need it. I expect money to grow. In return, I basically will ignore money and do whatever work pleases me without regard to remuneration."

Another person's explicit agreement with money might go like this: "I expect money to make me feel secure and provide me with the lifestyle I enjoy. In return, I will work hard to run my business properly." But the unconscious, irrational part of the agreement might be: "I expect money to destroy me. Because I feel so guilty and inadequate about taking over the business my mother worked hard to build while I just partied my way through life, I expect money to wreak vengeance on me. In return, I will do everything I can to prove I am inadequate, to sabotage the business, and in general to help money destroy me."

Although extreme, examples like these aren't that uncommon. Many people set up an agreement with money that perpetuates a cumbersome dependency on someone else, or extends a crippling control over another person. Many others set up agreements that are doomed to fail because they won't make the changes required to get the money they think they want.

How You Made Your Agreement: A Personal Money History

Your agreement with money began early in your life. It has evolved over the years, probably without your being aware of it. A good way to begin understanding your own agreement is to assess your personal money history.

Reflect back on your childhood. How much money did your family have? What was your family's style with money? As a child, what messages were you given about money? What

47

lessons were you taught? Who controlled the money? When did you start to have some? How did you use it? What were your financial ambitions?

In school and college, what were your goals? How did they evolve? In choosing a career, what role did money play? What did you *want* from money? What were you willing to do to get it?

In your personal relationships, how did money fit in? If you got married, what role did money play in your choice of a mate? Was your agreement with money modified? How does it differ from that of your spouse?

In your present life, what is your agreement with money? Are your feelings about money different from what they were when you were a child? Are they different from or similar to those of your parents? What themes concerning money have persisted since childhood? What are the irrational aspects of your current dealings with money?

In taking a personal money history, bear in mind that you will try to trick yourself into not telling the truth. Making this exploration with a sibling or an old friend can help guard against the universal tendency toward self-deception. But becoming aware of your agreement is only part of the task. The rest of the work lies in figuring out if it makes sense. Earlier, we saw how several destructive agreements— Sarah's, Rachel's, and Roger's, for instance—were formed. Now let's look at the formation of an agreement that does work.

A Sensible Agreement

The youngest of six children of an Italian-Irish family, Brian worked part-time from the fifth grade on. His father's job as a school janitor provided income for food, clothing, and shelter, but no extras. His mother worked part-time, as did all of the children, to make up the difference. From an early age, Brian thought of work as simply the natural way of things. His father, who liked his job, reminded his children frequently of two things: that after high school they would be on their own financially, and that to be happy in life you had to like your work.

Brian wasn't crazy about his paper route in the fifth grade, so he crossed that off his list of possible careers early on. But Brian did like to eat. When he returned home in the mornings he would go upstairs to his grandmother's apartment for breakfast; she was always baking something warm and delicious. By high school Brian was pretty fat. That got him a place at right tackle on the football team, as well as a lot of kidding at home, except from his grandmother, who thought fat was a sign of good spirits and good health.

Liking food and people, and not minding work, Brian decided to head for the restaurant business after high school. "Couldn't make a worse choice," his father said. "Ninety-nine out of a hundred fail."

He started as a dishwasher. His boss liked his willingness and interest, and he made a deal with Brian that he would finance cooking school if Brian would work part-time at the restaurant and for a year after he graduated.

By the time that year was up, Brian, who was making $7,500 a year, wanted to get married. The woman he wanted to marry, a waitress in the restaurant's cocktail lounge, made $8,000 a year. Between the two of them they thought they could swing it.

There was no doubt in Brian's mind that in time he would become the restaurant's chef and that eventually the opportunity would come along to have a place of his own. Two things stood in his way: money and experience.

He and his wife had a baby girl. His grandmother, now ninety-two, and his mother took care of her while the two worked. When the chef left for another job Brian took over.

His new ideas, picked up at cooking school, greatly improved the restaurant's reputation. Brian began to get job offers, but he wanted to learn more about the business before he made a move.

Finally, after eight years, the right offer came along at the right time—a partnership, to be purchased over time through his earnings, in a new waterfront location, backed by friends of the owner of Brian's current restaurant. After a slow start, the new place got written up by a national magazine and became one of the busiest restaurants in the city.

As for Brian's agreement with money, we can see it involved none of the substitution thinking of our other examples. He thought of money as a necessary, and procurable, means to an end. He respected money but didn't fear it. To get it, he was willing to work hard—at what he liked. He was unwilling to overwork frantically, to take on pointless jobs that couldn't help him and might burn him out. He believed that in time he would reach his goal, and he backed up that belief with rational action, not blind hope.

During his eight years of apprenticeship, Brian avoided falling into a low-level depression over money. The early years of working are a time when many people, particularly men, give up their dreams and fall into defeatism, which, of course, becomes a self-fulfilling prophecy. Brian also avoided the most common antidote to that defeatism—harebrained venturing: jumping into the first vaguely plausible deal that came his way.

Brian was able to do all that because he took care of himself psychologically (although he would be the last to express it that way). Equipped from childhood with a feeling of security and self-esteem, a belief that things can work out in life, he went after what he wanted calmly and surely. His agreement with money was not about power, love, or immortality. It was just about money.

The key to assessing accurately your agreement with

money is to probe its hidden or irrational components. Just as your agreement with your boss may include hidden wishes for power, control, or love, so may your agreement with money. That may be just fine, so long as the wishes are attainable and not self-defeating. Although money can certainly make you feel good, just make sure that your agreement doesn't include magical or substitution thinking and doesn't ask you or money to do things you or money can't do.

Part Two

MONEY STYLES

Seven

Style

Flamboyant and bold, timid and weak, inscrutable and hidden, frantic and obvious—everybody has a characteristic way of dealing with money. Rooted in your emotional makeup and the hidden meanings of money for you, your money style is as much an expression of your personality as the clothes you wear, the car you drive, the people you like. You are how you spend, in many ways.

As you read on about the most common money styles, you may see yourself in many of them—most of us are an amalgam. You should begin to discover your own individual money style. It may be helpful or destructive or both at once—many of the styles we describe have their advantages and disadvantages. But knowing how to work with your style, to use it to your advantage, can make a big difference in your life. For that reason we have provided for each style the case histories of people in the process of learning how to integrate their natural money style with rational financial decision-making. Following each profile is specific financial information of particular concern to that money style, and of general importance to everyone, no matter what your style.

What's Your Style?

The following quiz, although it has no real scientific validity, should help you identify your money style.

1. With which statement do you most agree?

   a. A penny saved is a penny earned.
   b. Nothing succeeds like success.
   c. Spend it now; you can't take it with you.
   d. Never mix business with pleasure.

2. On a Caribbean vacation you win a week's salary gambling. You:

   a. Wire it home so you can't touch it.
   b. Put it all on one bet.
   c. Set aside your original bet and plan to gamble the rest.
   d. Fritter it away on the island.

3. You see the perfect sweater, but it costs more than you have ever spent on a sweater. You:

   a. Buy it before your conscience says no.
   b. Ask them to hold it while you plan how to pay for it.
   c. Mutter some expression of outrage about how a store can charge so much for a sweater.
   d. Buy the sweater and return it the next day after looking at your bank statement that night.

4. After you leave a restaurant, your friend asks you why you left a tip even though a service charge was included. You:

   a. Go back and ask that the tip be returned.
   b. Feel annoyed with yourself, and walk on.
   c. Say, "What the hell, it's only money."
   d. Say, "He beat me out of it. More power to him."

5. In setting a fee for your services you typically:

   a. End up letting the fee be set for you or set a lower fee than you know you're worth.

b. Negotiate aggressively for the highest fee you can get.

c. Set an unrealistically high fee and hope for the best.

d. Set the fee and then feel you got taken.

6. Listening to a sermon about the evils of money, you:

   a. Feel guilty and uncomfortable.

   b. Wonder how the preacher spends his money.

   c. Resolve to do better.

   d. Agree and feel satisfied that you haven't been sucked in by money.

7. If you lost money in the Wall Street crash of 1987, your response was:

   a. Anger but determination to make it back.

   b. Doubling of your investments, thinking it was a good time to get in.

   c. Pleasure that you had so little invested.

   d. Self-admonition that you should have known better.

8. You inherit the equivalent of 5 percent of your annual salary from an unexpected source. You:

   a. Take a vacation and have a ball.

   b. Determine to take some risks to double the investment in one year.

   c. Put it in a retirement account.

   d. Put it in your checking account to pay bills.

9. With which statement do you most agree?

   a. Money is a scoreboard.

   b. Money is fun.

   c. Money is overwhelming.

   d. Money is toxic.

10. When it comes to decision-making in general, you:

    a. Go with your intuition and hope for the best.

    b. Procrastinate until forced to decide.

    c. Gather the facts and move fast.

    d. Avoid the downside above all else.

11. When it comes to insurance, you:

    a. Cover yourself to the maximum.
    b. Buy some insurance but don't really understand it.
    c. Pick and choose your spots, trying to keep costs to a minimum since you think insurance is a sucker's bet.
    d. Often go uninsured.

12. As for saving money you:

    a. Can't do it to save your soul.
    b. Have become very good at it through long experience.
    c. Make a new savings plan every other month.
    d. Have a fixed-deposit retirement plan but try to keep most free to invest.

13. Which of the following types of people turns you off the most?

    a. A pathological gambler.
    b. A whiner.
    c. An aggressive life insurance salesman.
    d. A self-righteous killjoy.

14. If you could choose one of the following occupations, regardless of income, which would it be?

    a. Writer.
    b. Airline pilot.
    c. Dancer or professional athlete.
    d. Judge.

15. The thing about money most people don't understand but you do is:

    a. How to protect it.
    b. How to make it.
    c. That it doesn't really matter.
    d. That you can't take it with you.

16. Which would you do with an unexpected free afternoon?

    a. Catch up on work.
    b. Go to a museum.

c. Raise hell.

d. Get the jump on the competition.

17. Which quality do you most admire in a person?

    a. *Joie-de-vivre.*
    b. Initiative.
    c. Imagination.
    d. Reliability and responsibility.

18. In terms of money, what is your hope for your children?

    a. To take it seriously before it's too late.
    b. To know that all it takes to make it is confidence and drive.
    c. That they have good luck.
    d. That they have knowledge and education.

19. What do you look for in a mate when it comes to his or her relationship with money?

    a. Stability.
    b. Ability to have fun with it.
    c. Ambition to make more.
    d. Not being too bothered about it.

20. Your Achilles' heel around money is:

    a. Ignorance.
    b. Inability to control it.
    c. Fretfulness.
    d. Feeling that you always have to make more.

21. Your worst realistic fear about money is:

    a. Putting yourself into overwhelming debt.
    b. Losing it.
    c. Not being able to make it.
    d. Losing out because you don't understand it.

22. An honest way to describe the way you drive a car is:

    a. Cautious, safe.
    b. Aggressive, safe.
    c. Fast, at times reckless.
    d. Nervous, on the alert.

23. If you had to go to one of the following, you would choose:

    a. A baroque concert.
    b. A Wagner opera.
    c. A Beethoven symphony.
    d. A Mahler symphony.

24. If you had to go to one of the following, you would choose:

    a. A baseball game.
    b. A football game.
    c. A golf tournament.
    d. A basketball game.

25. As for your bank balance right now:

    a. You're quite sure you know what it is.
    b. You know roughly what it is.
    c. You honestly don't know.
    d. You'd rather not think about it.

26. When it comes to tipping, you:

    a. Give the minimum, or if the service is bad, give less.
    b. Usually overtip.
    c. Reward good service with a big tip.
    d. Tip well even if the service is mediocre.

27. The statement you most agree with is:

    a. Hard work pays off.
    b. Neither a borrower nor a lender be.
    c. It's a dog-eat-dog world.
    d. All work and no play makes Jack a dull boy.

28. When you get a bank statement or other financial statement, you:

    a. Check it over carefully to the last penny.
    b. Usually can't figure it out.
    c. Toss it in a drawer and assume the bank was right.
    d. Go over it quickly, paying the most attention to the bottom line.

29. What word describes you best?

    a. Exuberant.
    b. Ambitious.
    c. Steady.
    d. Thoughtful.

30. What word describes you least well?

    a. Gloomy.
    b. Reckless.
    c. Cautious.
    d. Organized.

31. If you were a character in a book or a play, it would be written by:

    a. Ernest Hemingway.
    b. F. Scott Fitzgerald.
    c. Arthur Miller.
    d. Neil Simon.

32. A quality you admire in yourself is:

    a. You're always on time.
    b. You're not materialistic.
    c. You're a high-energy person.
    d. You're the life of the party.

33. A quality you're not proud of is:

    a. You're always late.
    b. You're materialistic.
    c. You pay too much attention to details.
    d. You have difficulty making decisions.

34. In college you majored in, or your major most resembled:

    a. English.
    b. Math.
    c. Economics.
    d. Dramatic Arts.

35. The person you'd most like to date, if he or she were independently wealthy, is:

    a. A schoolteacher.
    b. An artist.
    c. An editor at a publishing company.
    d. A management consultant.

36. The reason you don't have as much money as you want is:

    a. There aren't enough hours in the day.
    b. You're probably too cautious.
    c. You throw it away.
    d. You don't pay enough attention to it.

37. People who are tight with money are that way because:

    a. It makes sense.
    b. They're mean-spirited.
    c. They're scared.
    d. It's probably how they were brought up.

38. If you were ever to have an affair, it would be:

    a. A wild fling.
    b. A one-night stand.
    c. Well-planned and enjoyable.
    d. Something you got hoodwinked into.

39. In the kitchen you're:

    a. Frantic, messy, and creative.
    b. Disorganized and slow.
    c. Organized and surrounded by cookbooks.
    d. Organized, fast, and clean.

40. In terms of entertaining you like:

    a. Wild, spontaneous bashes.
    b. Cocktail parties.
    c. Well-planned dinner parties.
    d. Informal get-togethers with friends.

41. Spur-of-the-moment ideas:

    a. You almost always reject.
    b. Often get you into trouble.
    c. Are the best ones.
    d. Excite you.

42. Depression is usually the result of:

    a. A lack of energy.
    b. Some sort of failure.
    c. Some sort of loss.
    d. The inevitable cycle of things.

43. The best antidote to guilt is:

    a. Fixing up whatever you're feeling guilty about.
    b. Putting it behind you and moving on.
    c. Going out with other people and having some fun.
    d. Sleep.

44. What you don't know about money:

    a. Can't hurt you.
    b. You've got to learn.
    c. You'll deal with one way or another.
    d. Will catch you up one way or another.

45. Your attitude about borrowing from friends is:

    a. If you're fair they'll be fair.
    b. You should avoid it at all costs.
    c. Beware of terms that aren't clear.
    d. It can be dangerous because it's so easy.

46. When you think about retirement you:

    a. Wonder what you're going to do.
    b. Just hope things won't have collapsed by then.
    c. Can't imagine retiring.
    d. Can't wait for the party to begin.

Answer Key to Quiz

In the chart below, find the Key Letter, S, K, E, or U, to which each of your answers corresponds. If your answer to Question 1 was (a), circle the corresponding letter in the column labeled A, in this case, K. Then do the same for the rest of the questions.

	A	B	C	D
1.	K	S	E	U
2.	K	S	E	U
3.	S	E	K	U
4.	K	U	S	E
5.	U	E	S	K
6.	S	E	U	K
7.	E	S	K	U
8.	S	E	K	U
9.	E	S	U	K
10.	S	U	E	K
11.	K	U	E	S
12.	S	K	U	E
13.	K	E	U	S
14.	U	S	E	K
15.	K	E	U	S
16.	K	U	S	E
17.	S	E	U	K
18.	S	E	U	K
19.	K	S	E	U
20.	U	S	K	E
21.	S	K	E	U
22.	K	E	S	U
23.	K	S	E	U
24.	U	E	K	S

	A	**B**	**C**	**D**
25.	K	E	S	U
26.	K	S	E	U
27.	E, U	K	E	S
28.	K	U	S	E
29.	S	E	K	U
30.	E	K	S	U
31.	E	U	K	S
32.	K	U	E	S
33.	S	E	K	U
34.	U	K	E	S
35.	K	S	U	E
36.	E	K	S	U
37.	K	S	E	U
38.	S	K	E	U
39.	S	U	K	E
40.	S	E	K	U
41.	K	U	E	S
42.	S	E	U	K
43.	K	E	S	U
44.	S	K	E	U
45.	E	K	U	S
46.	U	K	E	S

Now add up the total number of S's and enter that number next to the S below. Repeat the same procedure for each letter, recording the total for each next to the corresponding letter below.

S =

K =

E =

U =

One letter's total should predominate over the others. Now look below to see which group matches that letter. Your dominant money style should be in that group.

Money Styles	*Meaning of Money*
S: The Spenders:	
Gambler	Action, Freedom
Manic	
Overspender	
K: The Skeptics:	
Pessimist	Security, Control
Worrier	
Miser	
E: The Enthusiasts:	
Jock	Power, Freedom, Self-Esteem
Hustler	
U: The Underinvolved:	
Victim	Anxiety, Dependency
Depressive	
Dodger	

Eight

What *Are* You Worth?

No matter what your money style, you should have a good idea of your net worth. It's surprising how many people don't really know. So, before discussing each money style in depth, let's get a picture of your personal balance sheet.

Depending on their psychological makeup, most people believe they're either richer or poorer than they really are. Some people fluctuate back and forth, depending on how they feel or what they are considering buying. It's not hard to convince yourself (or your banker) that you can afford something you really can't. On the flip side, an irrational fear of the poorhouse is just as easy to put over on yourself. Witness the person who cancels his favorite magazine subscription to save money and then buys an expensive painting.

If you don't already know, you should figure out exactly how much you *are* worth by filling out the following net worth worksheet. It's simple, takes only a few minutes, and most people are surprised by what they find.

A few instructions before you start: Assets are what you own. Liabilities are what you owe. If you own a house whose current market value is $300,000, that's its asset value. If there's a $150,000 mortgage on that house, that is a liability. Use the current market value when you are listing your assets.

Assets

Liquid Assets

Cash and checking accounts $_____

Savings accounts   _____

Life insurance cash value   _____

U.S. Savings Bonds   _____

Brokerage accounts   _____

Other   _____

    Total liquid assets $_____

Marketable Investments

Common stocks   _____

Mutual funds   _____

Bonds (corporate, municipal, etc.)   _____

Other   _____

    Total marketable investments   _____

"Nonmarketable" Investments

Business interests   _____

Investment real estate   _____

Pension, profit-sharing, etc. accounts   _____

Tax-sheltered investments   _____

    Total "nonmarketable" investments   _____

Personal Real Estate

Residence   _____

Vacation home   _____

    Total personal real estate   _____

Other Personal Assets

Auto(s)   _____

Boat(s)   _____

Furs and jewelry   _____

Assets (*Continued*)

Collections, hobbies, etc. _____
Furniture and household accessories _____
Other personal property _____
   Total other personal assets _____
      Total assets $_____

Liabilities

Current Liabilities

Charge accounts, credit card charges,
  and other bills payable _____
Installment credit and other short-
  term loans _____
Unusual tax liabilities _____
   Total current liabilities _____

Long-Term Liabilities

Mortgage(s) on personal real estate _____
Mortgage(s) on investment real estate _____
Bank loans _____
Margin loans _____
Life insurance policy loans _____
Other _____
   Total long-term liabilities _____
      Total liabilities $_____

Total assets $_____
Minus total liabilities $_____
NET WORTH $_____

The most common reaction of those figuring their net
worth for the first time is that they appear, on paper, to be

better off than they feel. Your reasons may be tied up in your emotions, but there may be rational reasons, too, such as ten years of rampant inflation in the 1970s.

The fact is that our feelings don't keep pace with our bank accounts. If you grew up poor, worked your way through college, and struggled to build up a business, your six-figure income may *look* like a lot, but you probably will still *feel* the way you did in college. In fact, it may take a few generations before the feeling of wealth settles in. This accounts for the common emotional differentiation between old and new money. That pattern can work the other way as well. It can take a few generations for the children of old money to lose their feeling of being rich even as the family fortune disappears.

This curious mind trick is similar to the situation of the person who grows up fat and then loses a lot of weight. That person may never feel thin and may never enjoy food without guilt. The components of our self-image are laid down early; it's very hard to alter its weave and shape in adulthood. Being a good athlete or a klutz, smart or stupid, fat or thin, funny or a bore, rich or poor—these are all components of our self-image, which adult reality alters only slightly. Remember your high school persona? How much of your current self-image is bound up in that? Even though you've changed so much, to a large extent you are still defined by that image as the real you, including how rich or poor you are, no matter what your balance sheet says.

How much money you can afford to spend obviously depends on many factors other than net worth. The liquidity of your net worth, your income, and your responsibilities to other people are the three most important factors affecting such decisions. A person with the majority of his net worth tied up in his house, with a low or unstable income and two children in college, is obviously more strapped than the single person with a high-paying job and a lot of liquidity, even though their net worth is the same.

Your net worth is an important figure, one that serves as a solid reality-based starting point for rational money management.

Now, chapter by chapter, let's approach each money style as it is, and as it could be. Remember, don't expect to see yourself in only one style. It's likely you will identify with aspects of several styles.

Nine

The Jock

The Jock, male or female, applies the values and methods of team sports, notably football, to dealing with life and with money.

The Jock wakes up in the morning hungry. He plans his day while he does his sit-ups. The Jock is psyched. He's up for the game. He believes in lining up with a good team, helping his teammates and expecting them to help him. He plays hard and he plays to win. He paces himself so that when the whistle blows he'll be ready. He talks it up with his teammates so that on game day they charge onto the field as a unit. He doesn't want to let his teammates down, so he thinks of them as he puts in his extra hours. If it weren't for money there would be no way of proving to his teammates how hard he's worked, how much he's worth to them.

Money typically becomes the goal, the scoreboard, the name of the game for the Jock, who knows that enormous potential is worth nothing unless it puts points on the board. Therefore, no matter how hard he works he will feel defeated if he doesn't make money. Although he may do great good in his work, if he doesn't make lots of money he will feel depleted. He needs a concrete answer to the question, "What are you worth?" The answer is, "I'm worth what I make."

The Jock usually has a coach—a boss, a father, a spouse, the memory of a certain figure—to egg him on. The coach will give him a kick when he needs it and a pat on the back when he needs that. The coach is always there, somewhere on the sidelines, never out of mind. He helps the Jock get psyched and helps him prepare, consoles the Jock through defeat and cheers him in victory. Wanting to please the coach, the Jock internalizes the coach's values—aggression and self-sacrifice—and carries them onto the field.

In going after money, the Jock is seldom passive or lazy. You don't want to pass up a big score. When it comes to investing, as with everything else in life, the Jock believes in the importance of a sound game plan, one that takes into account the strengths and weaknesses of the opposition. He believes in a balanced attack, a varied offense, conservative play as well as risk.

Two key qualities the Jock possesses—enthusiasm and hard work—fit very well into the competitive marketplace. The Jock knows that intellectuals mock him, but he doesn't appear to mind. He knows that he gets things done. As many lumps as he takes, he usually has fun. His persistence and optimism usually lead to financial success, which for him may be a redundancy. For the Jock, financial success is the *only* success.

The Jock is a particularly American phenomenon, one that draws smiles from the English and the French. But in terms of making money, his style usually works, as long as his stamina holds out. After you score, you tee it up and go for it again. You keep trying to score until time runs out—death, retirement, whatever. Most Jocks prefer making money to spending it. That's because the excitement lies in going for it, not in having or spending it.

The Jock's agreement with money goes something like

this: "If I work hard for money, money will give me the feeling of the camaraderie of competition I felt most when I was playing sports in school." His agreement is rational to the extent that the Jock's hard-driving, team-oriented style can make him a lot of money, and even provide some of the camaraderie he seeks.

One facet of the Jock personality, however, can lend itself to an irrational agreement that will defeat him. The Jock often has problems maintaining intimate relationships. If you're trying to get close to another human being it's difficult to be always driving for a touchdown. The go-for-it, hard-work, please-the-coach approach that works so well in business can be off-putting in romance. It can make for moments of great excitement, but over time the Jock discovers there is no end zone and no scoreboard. He begins to feel lost and awkward, and often his embarrassment leads him to tune out, to go back to the playing field, to get away from the more emotionally unpredictable realm of intimate relationships. Thus he often imposes upon money for something it simply cannot satisfy: the need for intimacy.

There are solutions to this problem. One is for a boy Jock to find a girl Jock. Two Jocks can grow old together, happily comparing notes on the latest game, maintaining a mutually agreed-upon distance. Or a Jock can find a mate who simply loves him as he is. Or a Jock can change and learn to enlarge his emotional repertoire.

The worst, and most common, solution is for the Jock simply to be happy at work and unhappy at home. At home he feels chronically devalued, misunderstood, and unappreciated. He feels defensive and always wants to tune out. At work he comes to life, feels excited, appreciated, connected with others. Obviously this pattern has a way of perpetuating itself.

Balancing Your Attack: A Sound Financial Lifestyle

Jack Ryan is a thirty-six-year-old marketing director for Technospeak, a computer software company in Silicon Valley. At work he's terrific at psyching his people up, creating an atmosphere of teamwork and thinking big. He makes $92,000 a year and has three children; his wife's part-time work as a substitute teacher adds another $18,000. The couple own a house in Menlo Park; their mortgage runs $1,220 a month. Part-time child care for their three young children takes another $7,000 a year of the Ryans' budget.

Jack's wife Barbara describes her husband as a workaholic and wishes he'd find more time to enjoy the good life they have. She's made an effort to learn more about what he does by becoming computer literate herself and wishes he'd consult her more often about financial decisions that affect both of them. Jack's friends and colleagues describe him as super-aggressive and competitive, but very loyal and friendly with those on his team. "Jack's the quarterback, no doubt about it," one of them says. "I just wonder when he sleeps."

As for Jack, his goals are simple: he wants more money. He and his family spend just about everything they earn. The Ryans have saved only the $2,250 a year Jack has put into their IRAs for the past six years. He doesn't worry much about that, though; he knows his hard-work approach will pay off.

The following list approximates the Ryans' monthly living expenses.

Taxes (federal, state, property)	$ 1,958
Mortgage on house	1,220
Child care	591

Automobile costs (two cars)	
(loans, insurance, maintenance)	533
Food at home	815
Vacations	500
Insurance policies	133
Consumer loans	366
House utilities and maintenance	600
Charitable contributions	250
Clothing	616
IRAs	187
Miscellaneous (unaccounted for) spending	1,530
Total	$ 9,299 a month
	$111,600 a year

Jack has two key psychological traits he should take advantage of in forging his optimum financial lifestyle: his love of teamwork and his aggressiveness. Let's look at how Jack can maximize his strengths and play down his weaknesses.

Jack says he wants to earn more money. He certainly has the personality for it. Like many Jocks, Jack is totally committed to his job, and he's winning the game. But is he getting the most out of what he puts in? If we take his stated goal at face value, there are ways he might reach that goal more quickly.

Jack might think about starting his own team. He wouldn't be the first team player to take what he's learned and go out and start his own franchise. Unconsciously, Jack may be avoiding that move because he doesn't want to hurt the coach—his boss—by competing with him and defeating him. For a lot of Jocks, loyalty makes them give up the best years of their careers playing down linemen when they could be running the team somewhere else.

That somewhere else might even include changing the game itself. Sales in software may not be nearly so lucrative as another field, like commercial real estate or securities. Using the same aggressiveness and capacity for teamwork,

Jack might make more money elsewhere. Team loyalty sometimes keeps Jocks in a rut.

What about saving more of that $111,600? At first glance,
there seems to be a lot of fat, but saving doesn't come easily
to a Jock. We're not surprised to see that Jack spends all his
money—he probably tries to give his family in money what
he deprives them of in time. If Jack won't mend his ways
emotionally, at least he can improve his family's material life
by changing the way he spends.

The House That Jack Builds

Jack might start by buying a better house. He and Barbara
can afford a mortgage of at least $2,000 a month based on
what they earn now. That change would not only help the
couple avoid letting their money dribble away on things they
don't need and only transiently want (the $1,530 a month
that they can't even account for), it would also be a good
investment as well as providing a nicer life for their family. If
Jack continues to spend all he earns, at least he would be
building up equity. When the day rolls around for his kids'
college tuitions he may be able to finance that with a home-
equity loan. On retirement he can sell his home, move to a
smaller house, and have money left over to invest and live on.

Because it's a long-term investment by its very nature,
because it usually requires monthly mortgage payments,
and because it's not all that easy to cash in quickly, real estate
can be an ideal investment for someone who would otherwise squander his money on things that don't add up to
much in the long run, or who would invade less liquid
investments in order to have money for nonessentials.

Investing in real estate might mean buying a first home
instead of renting, or buying a vacation house or rental
property. For Jack it might mean moving into a more expen-

sive house. Real estate also has certain tax benefits and is usually an excellent hedge against inflation.

The Team That Jack Builds

Assuming he does earn more and has more money for investments soon, Jack, like all Jocks, should begin to put together a financial team. He'll have fun—having meetings, talking on the phone, haggling over plans, going out for drinks, and making money. Starting with someone he knows and trusts—an old college friend, an athletic club buddy, a neighbor—his team should include a broker, a banker, a lawyer, and an accountant. The information his teammates give him will be less important than the team spirit they'll generate—that's what Jack needs to get himself going.

Starting His Team: The Broker

Jack will probably be happiest with a full-service broker. At its best, this kind of help gives you someone to bounce ideas around with who will look into strategies and specific investments for you. You can have fun and make money together. For many people, but particularly the Jock, the game itself becomes as enjoyable as the reward.

Why would anyone deal with a full-service retail broker when he (1) isn't objective because he works on a commission and makes more money the more you buy and sell; (2) can't document performance; and (3) isn't price competitive for the services he provides? The answer is, for a multitude of less tangible factors that are, for most investors, more important in the long run: familiarity, convenience, service, consistency, and the relationship that can develop between a client and broker.

Performance and price competition, within limits, turn

out to be less important to most people than you might think. The fact that you pay a full-service broker a 2 percent commission to buy a stock, for example, instead of 1 percent through a discount broker, usually makes very little difference in the long run. The investment either works or it doesn't. If the stock goes up 25 percent (and that possibility is the only reason to buy a stock in the first place), the commission hardly matters. The same is true with a 25 percent loss.

The novice investor, whatever his money style, can use a good broker for direction; the more sophisticated client often needs help on occasional special situations that only a full-service firm can handle: a block trade, tax swap, new issue, research information, tax advice.

There's no such thing as a typical investor, but let's take a look at another Jock, a successful full-service client who has made good use of the vast resources some brokers can provide.

The Advantage of a Good Financial Relationship

Barney, a doctor who plays squash with Jack, opened his first brokerage account in 1975 when he was the junior partner in a five-man radiology group. He was referred to his broker by another doctor. His first investment was a $15,000 municipal bond, which proceeded to fall in value for the next six years. But Barney embraces the Jock approach to investing. He's a good sport, a good team player, and he believes in working with experts.

Since then Barney has opened nine more accounts (a joint account, a pension, two IRAs, two custodian and two trusts for his children, and a Keogh), and through his yearly contributions and the generosity of the Great Bull Market, his combined accounts grew to over a million dollars at their peak in mid-1987. (The stock market itself, remember, tripled in value between 1982 and 1987.) In October 1987 his combined portfolios lost about 10 percent of their value. (About half his money was in stocks, which fell about 25 percent; the other half, mostly bonds, gained in value.) Over the years Barney has become good friends with his broker and has referred several of his colleagues to him. They talk on the phone every few weeks, and they get together four or five times a year. Barney is a long-term, loyal client.

In the first seven years of their association, Barney's broker didn't exactly make a fortune for him. It was hard to do well in any of the investments they were in: stocks, bonds, mutual funds, and occasionally options. But Barney never complained and never asked for a discount, even as his accounts grew in size. In 1980 his combined accounts dropped 11 percent in value as interest rates went through the roof (he was loaded with bonds). It didn't seem to make any difference that the accounts would have been worth slightly more if he had made the same investments through a discount broker. Barney believed the markets would eventually turn, and he was well positioned for that long, wild ride that started in 1982. In 1985 alone, his accounts appreciated 33 percent; no one cared that it might have been 34 percent by discounting.

In May 1986, Barney got paid back every nickel he had ever spent (or ever would spend) in fees. His broker had 1,500 shares of the hottest of the hot new issues—Home Shopping Network—to divvy up among his most loyal customers. He gave Barney 500 shares at the original offering price of 18. The opening trade was 42. Barney took his profit before the end of the year at 130, turning his $9,000 investment into $65,000. (The stock then proceeded to go to 282. At this writing, however, HSN sits humbly at 21. You should divide all these prices by 6, incidentally, to reflect two splits that the stock has had since it was issued.)

Red-hot issues don't come along often, but Barney has taken advantage of a multitude of other services. He saved money on insurance purchases through his broker. He bought a real-estate tax shelter in 1982 that lowered his taxes significantly for five years and then paid back his original investment. He and his partners financed some medical equipment through his broker at a lower interest rate than they were able to find at any bank. He's taken an equity loan on his house through his broker. He did a bond swap in December 1981 to lower his taxes. He set up a last-minute defined-benefit plan in 1986 that saved him a bundle in taxes that year. His broker has found lawyers and accountants for him and his friends when they've needed those specialists.

The overall consultative relationship and trust that develops over time becomes more important than quantitative performance and pricing figures for a Jock team player like Barney—or Jack. The resources that a very conscientious broker can offer are tremendous.

The Investments That Jack Builds

When he begins to invest Jack should first enhance his meager savings and investment scheme, perhaps by setting up a 401(K) or Keogh pension plan for himself. Jack should also pay particular attention to his children's approaching college tuitions.

Children are expensive these days. We've all seen those frightening estimates of what it will cost to get your baby from infancy through graduate school over the next few decades (arguably a million dollars per child, depending on what inflation factors you use and what kind of schools you plan on sending Junior to). And the new tax law takes some of the incentive out of building up an educational nest egg for your child during the early years. But there are still a few relatively painless things you can do to make the financial aspect of parenting less grim:

—Children under fourteen are now taxed in their parents' brackets, fourteen and older in their own. But there is still a small break for the under-fourteens: their first $500 per year of income is tax-free and their next $500 is taxed at their own rate. So if you have a $12,000 certificate of deposit paying $1,000 in interest each year (8.3 percent) in your own name and are losing 40 percent of that interest in taxes (i.e., 33 percent federal, 7 percent state), putting that CD in your child's name would save almost $400 a year with no effort at all. If you're not impressed with this saving, try compounding that or any other amount over eighteen years (birth to college) in your own bracket versus your child's (getting the $1,000 break until age fourteen and the larger break thereafter). The total nest egg in your child's name could be twice the size of yours by your taking five minutes to set it up that way in the beginning.

—Hire your child. So long as it's a legitimate job, you can shift income to your child's own tax bracket and take a business deduction at the same time. (It helps if you're self-employed or own a business.)

—You and your spouse can each give up to $10,000 a year to each child without incurring gift taxes. (There are no age limitations. For that matter, it doesn't even have to be your child.) A particularly logical gift to a tuition-needy child would be a stock that has appreciated significantly in value. If you sell it yourself, you'll have to deduct a hefty tax liability before sending that check off to Mount Holyoke. By giving the stock itself to your daughter, she can sell it, presumably incurring a lower tax before using the remainder for tuition. (The difference in federal taxes alone could be $3,600 on a $20,000 capital gain.)

Rooting for the Home Team

It's likely that Jack would find home less alien territory if he brought his team spirit home with him, if he invited his family onto the team. For instance, he seems to be leaving his wife out, and she's feeling it—the typical Jock's big mistake. Barbara certainly seems to want in on the action. But by retreating behind the sports pages and treating questions about his work as insincere or hopelessly naive, he's probably neglecting his greatest asset and staunchest ally. And as his children get older, Jack can involve them in their financial planning for college by letting them know what's going on. When it comes to money he can be his kids' coach.

If Jack can get the home team together they can have a lot of fun with money. The Jock's money lifestyle is a robust and affluent one. A big house, nice cars, clothes, vacations all add to the Jock's sense of self-esteem. The winning image he projects tends to make him more successful—financially, at least. The trick for the successful Jock is to find the time to *enjoy* his money and his personal life.

Ten

The Optimist

The Optimist brings to money the same attitude he brings to most situations in life: things will work out for the best.

The Optimist has a bit of Don Quixote in him and a bit of Peter Pan. He truly believes in the probability of a good outcome. His optimism typically withstands many assaults: silver linings are found in every cloud. Usually, this sunny attitude is unrelated to actual wealth. Some of the most optimistic people are financially poor.

Some people might call this attitude defensive: rather than endure the pain of seeing things as they are, the Optimist defends against the pain by looking only at the bright side. Or we might simply say that some people are just born happy.

Whatever the explanation, this attitude is hardy and durable. Because of his ability to take setbacks in stride, the Optimist is usually successful with money, as well as with other aspects of his life.

Consider Patty O'Donnell, a forty-three-year-old woman who lives in an Oregon resort community. When she married twenty-three years ago her husband was a fireman and she worked as a waitress until her two children were born. One day her husband was injured in a freak accident and paralyzed from the waist down. His disability insurance provided barely enough money to live on.

Patty wanted to stay home with her husband and children, but the family needed more money. Her husband became angry and bitter. Patty responded with sympathy and encouragement, which made him feel even worse. He attempted suicide. Throughout this ongoing crisis Patty never lost her conviction that she would find a way to make things better. The worse things got, the more determined she became.

As it happened, Patty was quite a skilled painter. She began selling her works. The local gallery started buying them, then the summer people started buying directly from her. Within a few years Patty had a thriving business, and her husband was a happy part of it.

The point of this story isn't that you can get rich as an artist, but that an optimistic money style can often beat the odds.

Less dramatic examples are legion. Many people remain quietly optimistic about money, treating it the way most of us treat the water supply. They know it could dry up, but they assume it will be there when they need it. They do the obvious things, like owning a house or having a savings account and a few investments, but by and large they don't worry about money. Their approach is one of benign respect: you do your work and I'll do mine. The well-adjusted Optimist knows that money is important, but he neither fears nor craves it. His financial status tends to follow the general economy; his happiness is minimally related to the rise and fall of his bank account.

The Optimist, trusting soul that he is, makes a cheerful agreement with money: "Come what may, you'll be there for me." Underlying that is something more complex: "I'm willing to go a certain distance to have you, but I don't want you to bring me any bad news." This, of course, leaves a lot of room for fate, or at least the economy, to play some nasty tricks.

Take this agreement just a bit further, and you discover its irrational side, namely, "If I ignore the bad news it will go away." Revealed in this is an underlying feeling of powerlessness. The pitfall for an extreme Optimist is that he may, in the face of important financial warnings, become so upset by the bad news that he chooses to disregard it altogether. Unable to deal rationally with signs of financial trouble, he simply says, "It will all work out." When this approach becomes broadly defensive it can be disabling.

Lining Clouds with Silver: Toward a Sound Financial Lifestyle

Martin Lewis is a forty-nine-year-old pediatrician who lives in rural Texas with his wife and four children. He is a jovial, bow-tied, rotund little man who looks larger than life to the families he treats. Speeding around in his red MG, he works endless hours. His energy and cheerfulness, his willingness always to be where he's needed have made him one of the most popular doctors in the state. "He's a throwback to the old-fashioned doctor," says one parent. "My kids actually look forward to going to see Dr. Marty," says another.

Now that the children are older, his wife Susan, a nurse, runs his office, and she complements his ebullience with a reassuring air. Since they met when Marty was in medical school at Tulane, they have shared a vision now realized: a big, happy family and dedication to treating sick children. Sustained by their ideals, an unshakable optimism, and an absolute faith that good work will be rewarded, the couple has preserved a happy marriage despite their long hours of work.

Along the way Marty and Susan have paid little attention to money, simply believing that with hard work things will work out okay. Susan takes care of the books, Marty brings in the money, and although many bills go uncollected the Lewises have done very well. All the kids are in a private high school. They have a big, sprawling house and two cars. They aren't extravagant, but it's taken a considerable income just to keep things going.

The problem is that Marty and Susan never anticipated the financial pinch educating four kids would create. The bull market of the eighties buoyed Marty and pumped in the extra cash he needed for private school tuition. But when the market dropped in October 1987, Marty's investments fell by 30 percent, and suddenly the extra money he had counted on for the kids' college costs was gone.

His initial reaction was to pretend it hadn't happened, but Susan wouldn't let him. "We can't just borrow more, Marty. We've already mortgaged the house twice and who knows how much more we owe. We need help."

"But honey," Marty argued, "things will work out. They always have."

Susan prevailed upon Marty to sit down with her brother, a lawyer in Austin, to go over their situation.

What they found was that their situation wasn't as bad as it might have been, but that without some careful planning the college tuitions would just about bust them, or at least ruin any chance they might have of a decent retirement income. The first step for Marty and Susan was to learn about loans and debt management.

Getting into Debt

Loans are simple transactions—a way of buying money on time. The borrower promises to repay the lender the amount he's borrowed (the principal) over a certain length of time (the term), normally also paying the lender an additional percentage of the borrowed amount (interest). The higher the interest, the higher the cost of the money you're buying on time. In a secured loan the borrower gives the lender the right to take a piece of his property (the collateral) if the borrower doesn't repay (defaults on) the loan according to the agreement.

For fast and uncomplicated loans, there are several places to look. Here are four that require collateral and three that require only the lender's faith in your creditworthiness.

Secured Loans

Home-equity loans have become big business since the 1986 Tax Reform Act, because they're one of the relatively few remaining tax-saving loans (the interest is deductible from your income). Every bank, savings and loan, and brokerage house in town is pushing home-equity loans, so rates are competitive. Typically, you can borrow up to 80 percent of the net equity (the value of your home less any mortgages) in your home at an interest rate that fluctuates at approximately 1 percent above the prime rate. It's a low-risk loan for the lender, who has a claim on your house if you default, and a low-cost loan for you.

This kind of loan is not instant money, however. Getting your house appraised and other application procedures can sometimes take a few months. But once the loan is approved you can write yourself a check whenever you need money. (Typically, home-equity loans offer you a line of credit—you pay interest only on what you use of the amount available to you.) Most of these loans, incidentally, can also be made to the owner of a rental property.

The danger of home-equity loans is that they are so relatively easy to get, and that they give the owner easy access to what might be his only safe and untapped savings.

Many people today are trying to figure out whether or not they should use home-equity loans to make other kinds of investments, such as in securities. They have a lot of equity built up in their houses and feel they should be putting that money to work.

Unfortunately, the answer to this question lies solely in the outcome of the investment you make with the proceeds of your loan. If you buy stocks or a mutual fund there's no way to know how you'll do. If the cost of the money is 10 percent you'll have to make more than 10 percent in the market with your borrowed money to come out ahead. (The interest on the loan is tax-deductible. The capital gains are taxable.) And keep in mind that home-equity loans are not at fixed rates. If interest rates rise the risk is double-barreled: not only does your carrying cost increase, but your stocks (and especially bonds) will likely lose value at the same time because of the rising interest rates.

Whole-life insurance policies may be borrowed against at a very low rate, usually 6 percent. The cash value built up on your policy depends on how long you've had it and on the amount of its benefit. If you have a policy that goes back a number of years, you may be pleasantly surprised. Because the insurance company doesn't exactly remind you about this low-rate loan, call your agent to find out how it works.

Brokers' margin loans are available against most securities, including mutual funds as well as stocks and bonds. Rates are based on a small markup over the broker call rate (the rate at which the broker borrows the money) and the paperwork is minimal. You just deposit your securities, sign what's called a margin agreement, and ask for a check. Pay it back when and if you want to. As long as your broker has your securities and they don't decline in value too much, he doesn't care if you keep your loan forever and never make an interest payment. The interest simply accrues against your account. Keep in mind that buying securities on margin increases your risk as well as your potential return. After the 1987 market crash many investors got the dreaded "margin call" from their broker—asking for more money or collateral to support accounts that had lost value overnight.

Company savings plans, profit-sharing plans, and 401(K) plans can be good sources of credit for those fortunate enough to be vested in them. Check with the benefits manager at your company.

Unsecured Loans

Your bank, savings and loan, or credit union may make a personal, unsecured loan if you are creditworthy. With the advent of overlapping financial services in the 1980s, these three institutions are essentially in the same business, so rates are generally competitive.

Finance companies, such as Beneficial Finance, Household Finance, and hundreds of smaller ones, specialize in making higher rate loans to less creditworthy customers. It's more important to compare loan rates among these companies because the differences are greater. And be sure you deal with a reputable company.

Friends and family may lend you money if you're in a bind, but be sure you don't lose a friend over a misunderstanding about money. Draw up a simple written agreement—a promissory note—stating the exact terms of the loan. You can find these forms in most stationery stores, or you can simply draft your own.

Even if it all looks straightforward, be aware that when you borrow from friends and family you may incur far more than just a financial debt. By the same token, be aware that when you lend you may be letting yourself in for something worse than losing some money. Patterns of pathological dependency and guilt, for example, can be perpetuated in families through the borrowing and lending of money. If you're a Victim's friend or relative (see Chapter 17), for instance, bear in mind that the borrower really may need a "no," rather than the "yes" that perpetuates his role as Victim. Similarly, by lending money, the family and friends of a Gambler (see Chapter 12) can "enable" him (to use a phrase from AA) to continue his habit.

Some people find it extremely difficult to borrow from friends or family. The act of asking for money, particularly from a person who is not inclined to give it, can generate feelings of humiliation and pain.

The act of asking for money generally implies that you're not in control, not grown-up, somehow not as good as the person from whom you're asking to borrow. Women, in financial distress because their former husbands have stopped paying support, often develop other problems that decrease their self-esteem. Having to ask for money does nothing to raise their sense of self-worth.

In some families the scene becomes a sadistic ritual. You ask for, say, $10,000, and it's doled out in $2,000 increments, each of which must be begged for and each of which is accompanied by criticisms of the borrower's financial habits. "How much did you spend on that vacation? Don't you think you could cut back here? What's wrong with the car you have now? This is money, you know."

Just as animals sometimes attack and kill the wounded member of the pack, adult humans often attack and humiliate people in financial trouble. Behind the facade of a cooperative financial discussion between friends or family members, a ritual of human disgrace is often acted out. From the initial encounter to the payback schedule, it's often hard for the borrower to preserve his self-respect.

How Much Debt Is Too Much?

America is a nation of debtors. We thrive on the spend-now-pay-later system of credit. The average American household spends about 75 percent of its after-tax income servicing its debt, while saving only 2 percent.

If no emotions about money or debt were involved, it would be fair to say that as a general rule high leverage (high debt) as a spending and investment strategy works well in times of high inflation, particularly if the inflation rate exceeds that of a fixed-rate loan. Anyone who bought a house with an 8 percent tax-deductible mortgage in the 1970s and saw that house's value increase by 15 percent a year tax-free, had a great investment as well as a nice place to live. In the late 1970s and early '80s, with double-digit inflation, borrowing tax-deductible money that could be repaid in the "cheaper dollars" of the future made sense, even if you were using the money to buy consumer products. With prices always on the rise, there was little incentive to save money for any future purchase.

But this way of thinking leaves a lot to be desired during periods of low inflation, especially with today's restrictions on the tax deductibility of consumer debt. Does it make sense to borrow at 10 percent, non-tax-deductible, to buy something that may cost only 3 to 4 percent more next year?

Even in buying a house, the one area where leverage always seemed to work, a lot of people have been trapped in recent years. If you bought a condominium in Miami for $150,000 five years ago with 90 percent financing and find that its market value now is only $125,000, guess what? You don't own anything. Your equity has been wiped out. In fact, you're making payments on something on which you have $10,000 negative equity ($125,000 value minus $135,000 debt). Thousands of homeowners have come to this very realization in such weak housing markets as Miami, Houston, and the Southwest, and have simply walked away from their purchases. They were overleveraged with a bad investment.

Carrying too much debt is the most common cause of (in fact, the very definition of) personal bankruptcy and financial ruin. Short of bankruptcy, the effects of debt can still be devastating, ranging from loss of self-esteem to broken marriages. Credit is so readily available today that debt addiction is an easy habit to get into. Credit cards are being pushed on us everywhere we turn. Home-equity loans are easy and convenient, yet most people who use them are tapping into their sole bastion of financial security.

Is all borrowing evil, then? Of course not. Most of us have to carry some debt, and at times there are investment opportunities available that make borrowing as much as you can get probably the smartest thing to do.

How do you decide how much debt you can handle and whether or not to add any more debt? First, you have to decide how much you want what you're thinking about buying. Emergency borrowing is obviously the highest priority. Indeed, it's wise to have a line of credit available to draw on in case of an unexpected medical expense or family emergency. The next most justifiable reasons to borrow are for two necessary, commonly leveraged items: a house or a car. Ninety percent of all homes are bought with some sort of financing, and 65 percent of all cars are financed. Other commonly financed expenses are college and graduate school tuitions, home improvements, and furniture. Luxury items must be put into another category.

To figure out whether or not you can handle more debt, first determine your annual cash flow. Here's how Marty and Susan figured theirs, using numbers rounded to the nearest $1,000:

Earned Income

Gross receipts from practice	$175,000

Investment Income

Stock dividends	2,000
Taxable interest	3,000
Tax-free interest	4,000
Rental property income in excess of debt service	9,000
Total	$ 18,000
All Income	$193,000

Because most of this money is already spoken for, however, let's figure out how much excess disposable income they have (again, using round numbers).

Marty's Practice	*Annual Cost*
Office rent	$ 12,000
Malpractice insurance	12,000
Secretary	16,000
Nurse (Susan)	22,000
Utilities	4,000
Equipment	5,000
Pension contribution	20,000
Miscellaneous	3,000
Total office	$ 94,000

Family Expenses

Taxes	$ 22,000
Mortgage	12,000
Automobile costs	6,000
Food at home	10,000
Vacations	7,000
Insurance policies	2,000
Consumer loans	4,000
House utilities and maintenance	10,000

Charitable contributions	5,000
Clothing	8,000
Total family	$ 86,000
Total income	$193,000
Minus total fixed expenses	$180,000
Disposable income	$ 13,000

Whether or not you should take on more debt depends on how much leverage you can stand. Most financial planners would tell you that your mortgage payments should not exceed 30 percent of your cash flow, and that your total non-mortgage installment payments should not exceed an additional 20 percent of cash flow. But it really depends on a multitude of factors. What assets you own probably is the most important. If you have a nice little nest egg of securities, deferred compensation, rental properties or other assets tucked away somewhere for the future, you can feel much more comfortable carrying a higher percentage of debt than if you didn't have such assets. Also, your age, tolerance for risk, and the security and future of your career income have an impact on how much debt you should carry.

Marty and Susan are fortunate to be in a position to increase their debt if they need to: they have a highly secure income and considerable assets. Their current debts total only about one-third of their net worth. Marty and Susan's assets look like this:

	Current Market Value
House (owned for 18 years)	$ 420,000
Two rental properties	
(house and apartment nearby)	465,000
Pension/profit-sharing plan	
(mostly stocks and bonds)	510,000

	Current Market Value
Nonpension cash and securities (stocks, bonds, mutual funds, money market funds)	120,000
Personal property (cars, furniture, etc.)	100,000
Total assets	$1,615,000

Against these assets, the Lewises have mortgages and consumer debt totaling $405,000. Their current net worth, therefore, is $1,210,000. Yet only $120,000 of this is liquid. Marty has a gross annual income of $175,000. But after covering the costs of running his practice, contributing to his pension, paying taxes, and paying for fixed family expenses, he is left with only about $10,000 to $20,000 a year of personal savings.

The Lewises are looking at something like $272,000 to get their four children through college over the next ten years (four children at $17,000 a year), and God forbid if any of them wants to go to medical school.

They could sell one of their properties, but being Optimists, they believe real-estate prices in Texas will rise again and they want to hold on. Marty could work harder, but not to the tune of saving an extra $25,000 a year after expenses and taxes.

A man with Marty's income and net worth could borrow money from any of the sources described in this chapter: against his house, insurance policies, or securities, for example. But in looking at his balance sheet we can see that the pension plan they so wisely set up years ago stands out as the largest untapped source of borrowing power. It also has two distinct advantages: he sets the terms, and he pays himself interest. They'll have to pay themselves (the pension) a fair interest rate for borrowing this money, but they shouldn't mind doing so: the interest is tax-deductible from their personal income and tax-free to the pension. And they'll be able to wait for the market to come back up on their depressed real-estate investments.

It may not seem like much of a problem for a millionaire like Marty to put his kids through school. But many middle-aged professionals find themselves in his predicament: high net worth but relatively little liquidity and tremendous expenses coming up fast. In Marty's case, only 10 percent of his net worth is liquid. And those total liquid assets—$120,000—are less than half of what he'll need to get his kids through college over the next ten years. He has to borrow or liquidate.

By anticipating the problem, Marty and Susan are protecting themselves from the Optimist's tendency to hide from unpleasantness. And they can continue to live with their agreement with money: If I treat you well you'll treat me well.

Debt Crisis

If you find yourself making late payments on your loans you had better act quickly to cut back on your spending. The obvious areas to cut back on are luxury items and credit card charges. This is easy to say but excruciating to do, in part because it exacerbates your feelings of guilt about how much your irresponsibility has already cost you, in part because cutting back arouses precisely those feelings of deprivation you have been trying to avoid.

Dangerously high debt can precipitate a genuine emotional crisis, and you should treat the crisis as just that. If your debt is seriously out of control you may want to go to what is called a credit counselor for help. Be careful of most commercial operations in this area; they end up charging you a fat fee for simply strapping you with more debt. They have fancy names for their services, like "debt consolidation" (wrapping all your loans together in a single loan that they arrange) or "credit repair shops" (which get you new credit cards). Both are like giving a drink to an alcoholic.

But there is one place that might really help. It's called the National Foundation for Consumer Credit (8701 Georgia Avenue, Silver Spring, MD 20910; [301] 589-5600). This organization can direct you to one of 250 nonprofit services that deal with chronic personal debt problems. The foundation is financed by the American Bar Association, the Legal Aid Society, several banks and other organizations. You will be asked to fill out a questionnaire about your credit problems. Then a credit counselor will talk to you about setting up a better cash flow budget and a debt repayment plan. This person can also contact your creditors for you if you wish.

Eleven

The Hustler

Wherever there's a buck to be made is where the Hustler wants to be. By "hustler," we mean not a con man or cheat, but the person who's always on the alert for a deal, an angle, a scheme.

Money excites the Hustler. Like the Jock, he enjoys having it, but even more than the Jock does, he loves to make it. He's often someone who grew up poor or insecure, and nowadays he is often a she. The kick of making money adds a whole new dimension to increasing the self-esteem of many women, as it's been doing for men for centuries. At its best, the Hustler's style is direct, energetic, and unapologetic. Freed from any sense of restriction, the Hustler can unabashedly go for it.

The Hustler may be Horatio Alger, but he may also be in danger of becoming Ivan Boesky. He often has an "I'll show them" attitude, and money is what he'll show them with. With money he will repair that sense of the-odds-are-against-me; with money he will show those people who thought he wasn't good enough. The opposite of the Victim, the Hustler hates the dependent position and will fight for his independence. His means to that end is money.

The Hustler's attitude toward money is one of dogged determination: "People may not respect me, but they do respect money." He says to money: "I know you're hard to get, but I'm going to get you. If I work hard, if I hustle, you'll fix me up." The Hustler's rational agreement is that hard work will lead to money and that money will provide all the good things it can buy. That makes perfect sense. In its irrational aspect, though, the agreement goes like this: "The money I get from my hard work will take care of all the other emotional conflicts I have that have nothing to do with money."

The Hustler can get so hooked on making money that he thinks of nothing else. If his drive comes from a desire to show the people who put him down in the past, that drive may turn into a need to take revenge. If his drive comes from low self-esteem, what began as a refreshingly feisty, hardworking, and clever person becomes insatiable. What began as need becomes greed.

So long as the Hustler doesn't go off either of those deep ends, his style can be an exciting and fulfilling approach to money and life. Combining optimism with vigilance and hard work usually produces positive results.

The Icarus

The mythical Icarus flew too close to the sun, which melted his wings and sent him crashing to his death. It's a tricky business deciding how high is too high, what's merely clever and what's illegal. For most people, there comes a time when they say, "This is high enough," or, "It's not worth the risk." Others, though, are so determined to test the hypothesis of their own omnipotence, they proceed until they're caught.

The modern Icarus has achieved wealth but has become so dependent on making money for power and self-esteem that he begins to take reckless, often illegal risks in order to make more and more. When one of them makes the headlines, most people are puzzled. Why would someone who had so much . . . ? The point is that the Icarus has so little.

Sometimes the Icarus is born of the very headiness of getting away with financial or legal murder. He becomes very serious, even grim, as he considers the possibilities. Slowly the idea begins to take form that there is no limit. Rules are bent, then broken; then there are no rules at all. Occasionally the Icarus is someone who felt all along that he was special, that the rules didn't apply to him.

The ancient Greeks attributed this pattern to hubris, the sin of pride. Current psychiatric thinking would speak of the Icarus in terms of sociopathy or narcissism. The socio-path has no conscience and so feels permission to break all rules. The narcissist feels a special sense of entitlement, as if the laws were suspended in favor of him, or as if the law enforcers were too stupid to catch him. Beneath the sense of entitlement there is usually an achingly low self-esteem, which the narcissist bolsters with his proclamation, "I am special." There is some of that in all of us to be sure, but the Icarus takes it to an extreme. For his extreme pain, the pain of not liking himself, he seeks extreme remedies.

The evolution of such a personality can be without marked trauma but usually includes insufficient nurturing in the early years. Because what he got as a child wasn't enough, the narcissist has to make up for that by getting from others, through high achievement (a legitimate means) or through exploiting others, as in the Icarus.

The Icarus' destructive agreement with money is: "If I risk it all for you, you will take me beyond the limits of mortal man." This agreement is not destined to work, yet these people fascinate us. For all our disapproval of what they do, we see them as testing a part of ourselves we would like to test. Even as we watch them fall we marvel at their daring. Most of us would like to outstrip our ordinariness, our mortality. Few of us ever get close enough to such heights to entertain the possibility seriously. Of the few who do, not all have the dignity and self-control not to follow the Icarus flight pattern.

The Lone Ranger Rides Again: A Sound Financial Lifestyle

Chip Holmes, a forty-two-year-old real-estate investor, lives in Washington, D.C. He's a self-made millionaire who got that way by hustling. Unlike his counterpart, Jack Ryan the Jock, Chip isn't a teamwork type but a private and introverted man. His father was manic-depressive, often hospitalized in mental institutions, and Chip grew up poor and angry. The pain of his father's illness and the ridicule Chip felt made him an intensely ambitious man with a tendency to keep to himself.

For Chip, making money became a means of conquest, of taking revenge. The money would give him the power and respect of which his father's mental illness had deprived him. He set his mind to it early and made a vow to himself: "I *will* be rich." Luckily, he had a knack for making money and found the competitive world a real turn-on.

While working his way through college, Chip became very interested in real estate. At first, because he didn't have a dime to his name, he located and negotiated properties for other investors. Soon he had enough money to start flipping contracts and doing small deals of his own. Over the next ten years he made a fortune: buying and selling, buying and holding, syndicating properties, converting apartment buildings into condos, getting into land development and construction, and rezoning urban areas. Chip, in short, became spectacularly successful simply by capitalizing, as he puts it, "on the good part of what my father left me: a crazy mad-dash way of running at life."

Chip's first marriage ended in divorce, largely because he was never home. Now remarried and the father of two young children, he balances family and work much better than before. His happiness at home, in fact, has led him to question whether he should continue driving himself so hard.

Using very well-rounded numbers, this is what Chip's balance sheet currently looks like:

Assets

Six commercial properties	$35,000,000
Stocks and bonds	800,000
House	500,000
Art collection	500,000
Personal property	
Two cars	40,000
Antiques	200,000
Jewelry	50,000
Oriental rugs	50,000
Total assets	$37,000,000

Liabilities

Mortgages on properties	$22,000,000
Margin debt on stocks	250,000
Mortgage on house	120,000
Tax liabilities on future sales of properties	3,000,000
Total liabilities	$25,000,000
Net worth	$12,000,000

Chip's problem, if we can call it that, is that he's about to sell the largest of his properties, his share in a shopping mall that he got into eleven years ago. It will free up almost $6 million, about half his net worth. But the decision to sell this property, precipitated by a disagreement with one of his partners, has brought about a kind of Hustler's identity crisis.

On the one hand, his mind is automatically percolating

the usual investment questions: Should I roll this money into more real estate or is it time for securities now? Are we heading toward inflation? How much should I leverage?

Those are easy questions for Chip, almost a relaxation. But the bigger picture perplexes him. If, at this point, he liquidated all his real-estate holdings he could produce a tax-free income of almost a million dollars a year by investing in municipal bonds, and perhaps change the focus of his life. He has thought about getting involved in public service. On the other hand, he believes that he stands a chance now of making really big money in his lifetime, leaving a legacy to his family for generations to come.

This kind of money "problem," which most of us can only fantasize about, leads to other money lifestyle questions for Chip. When most of his money was tied up in real estate he could pretend he wasn't all that rich. Now when he ponders liquidating half, or perhaps all of his equity, he is concerned about some practical implications of really being rich.

How secretive should he be? A part of him would like to splash his money all over town, for his own ego and his father's. Another part of him doesn't want to call attention to himself at all. He enjoys his privacy, and he doesn't want to stir up envy and resentment in his friends. The prospect of having so much cash is even making him slightly paranoid, especially about the IRS. He has fantasies about taxes slowly gouging his money out of him. And his bad experience with his partner makes him wonder if he can trust anyone now. It is common for Hustlers to have problems in partnerships or groups. They are individualists at heart.

In dealing with these problems Chip has many options, the bedeviling blessing of the rich. A friend of his, an investment banker, thinks that Chip should diversify his holdings more at this time, instead of concentrating so much in real estate. He talks about turning over some of his money to one of the New York investment advisory firms so that Chip wouldn't have to be so actively involved with that part of his assets.

Investment Advisers: The Blind Leading the Blind?

A registered investment adviser is someone who manages a lump sum of money for you, usually on a discretionary basis and usually for a fee based on the amount of the assets under management. The portfolio's objective can be income or growth, or a combination of the two. In a way it's like a personalized mutual fund.

Investment advisers, also known as money managers or portfolio managers, are typically Optimists. They have to be, since they live and die by their performance records. They are famous for focusing on the half of the glass that's full. In a good performance year they make sure the whole world knows about it. After a bad year they tend to say, "One year's performance means nothing. We're long-term investors."

Hiring a portfolio manager makes a lot of sense for large individual investors or for fiduciaries of other people's money (e.g., pension money) who don't want the direct responsibility of handling their investments. Anyone with less than about $100,000 is better off with mutual funds, which are cheaper, simpler, and more liquid (undoing a whole portfolio when you switch managers is expensive), and are much more standardized in performance measurement. Most investment advisory companies have a minimum of $250,000 to a million dollars.

Even considering an investment adviser, of course, assumes the investor's willingness to take the risk inherent in stocks and bonds. (For highly secure or very short-term bonds, one doesn't need to bother with hiring a portfolio manager.)

For the larger, more sophisticated investor, portfolio management seems to have three distinct advantages over the traditional broker-client system of stock investing: objectivity, performance orientation, and price competition.

The cost of using an adviser is twofold: a percentage of the assets' fee (usually 1 percent a year for under a million dollars) and brokerage commissions. You can use your own broker or let the adviser make the transactions where he wants. Because they are concerned with net results in your portfolio and don't benefit from commissions themselves, most investment advisers look for vastly discounted rates. Small independent advisers often use discount brokers; large advisory networks usually use full-service institutional brokers at even greater discounts.

Finding an Investment Adviser: How to Tell the Pros from the Cons

There are now approximately 15,000 SEC-registered investment advisers to choose from. They include major independent advisory firms, divisions of mutual fund companies, brokerage firms, and trust departments of major banks, as well as hundreds of one-person operations all over the country. The major players measure their assets in billions; the retired accountant may be managing a few million dollars for some of his former tax clients. Don't be too impressed by the "SEC-registered" part: if you have the $150 registration fee and haven't been convicted of securities fraud recently, you can be registered too.

How do you find a good investment adviser? You can conduct the search yourself, or you can hire someone in the burgeoning investment advisory consulting business to do it for you. (As if having thousands of new advisers to choose from isn't confusing enough, there are now thousands of new consultants to help you pick the right adviser.)

Doing It Yourself

The first step is to narrow your field by getting an objective report on performance. One of the largest advisory search companies sells its performance list for a reasonable price: CDA Investment Technologies, Inc. 1355 Piccard Drive, Rockville, MD 20850. For $175, CDA will send you a survey of the 360 investment advisers it monitors, showing their performance going back as far as ten years. It will also monitor the adviser you select and send you a quarterly performance report for an additional fee.

Many investors feel that the single most important question about equity (stock) managers is simply this: Who most consistently beats the Standard & Poor 500 Index through good and bad market cycles? Once you've identified several top performers whose minimum account size fits your portfolio size, write for their material. After reading it, interview each one by phone and invite three or four to visit your office before making a final selection.

Bear in mind, however, that it's much more difficult to monitor and rank investment advisers than, say, mutual funds. The industry is famous for creative accounting methods when it comes to stating quarterly performance figures. Nothing is standardized. Some firms have several individual managers, each performing differently, each with many different accounts with their own objectives and requirements.

Using a Consultant to Find an Adviser

There are two kinds of consultants who would love to help you find and then monitor your investment adviser: those who want to charge you a fee and those who want to get your brokerage commissions. Fee-based consultants are considered more objective than broker-consultants, but they tend to specialize in larger-scale pension business.

Fee-based consultants: You can hire an investment advisory consultant to help you work up a set of realistic investment objectives, present you with a selection of advisers with good records, and schedule interviews for you. The same company will usually monitor your adviser's performance and send you a comprehensive quarterly performance evaluation for about $500 a year.

CDA can recommend a consultant that uses their data system. There are also two trade associations of fee-based advisory consultants, either of which would be happy to send you a list of members:

> Investment Management Consultants Associations
> 3545 South Tamarac
> Denver, CO 80237

> The Institute for Investment Management Consultants
> P.O. Box 2722
> Carefree, AZ 85377

Broker-consultants: The ranks of broker-consultants swelled in the bull market almost as fast as the ranks of regular stockbrokers did. In fact, many of them are the same people: stockbrokers in the morning and consultants in the afternoon. Using a broker-consultant is fine if he specializes in this work, if his brokerage commissions are at least reasonably competitive, and if he is truly an objective consultant.

Objectivity may be the hardest quality to come by. Some broker-consultants try to steer their prospective customers toward the asset management divisions of their own companies, toward advisory companies that split their management fees with the broker who brings in the customer, or toward advisers who they know will trade more actively than others.

Some broker-consultants recommend what is called a wrap-fee: a 2 to 3 percent annual charge that covers the selection of an adviser, brokerage commissions, and a nice quarterly performance report on how the adviser is doing. This arrangement is very expensive when you compare it to the component values of each service.

Spreading the Wealth

Like many Hustlers looking to balance their lives better, the best route for Chip might be to create a compromise. Since half of Chip's net worth remains tied up in real estate— illiquid, highly leveraged, and at risk—perhaps Chip could add security and enjoyment to his life by realigning the other half of his assets:

House: Paying $2 million for a house might seem ridiculous, unless you have $10 million more, like Chip. It might even turn out to be a good investment. He and his wife have always talked about their dream house, and they can afford it if that's what they want.

Personal property: Chip already has a $500,000 art collection that he's very proud of. He could certainly afford to add to his collection, increasing his total personal property (including antiques, furnishing, jewelry, etc.) to $1 million. The art, if bought wisely, could also be a good long-term investment.

Stocks: Fortunately, Chip didn't have much money in the stock market in October 1987. A daring contrarian, he started taking some positions soon after, however, hand-picking several blue-chip companies. He could certainly afford to double his current $800,000 portfolio of good-quality stocks and bonds for long-term growth and income.

Because Chip now has a large lump sum to invest, he might consider hiring two investment advisers, giving each one half of his equity money and making them compete with each other.

Trusts: If he doesn't already have trust accounts set up for his children Chip should see his lawyer and get started. He might start with $500,000 for each child. The securities in his children's accounts should be even more conservative than his own: a mix of zero coupon bonds (see page 125), Treasury instruments, and money market funds, as well as blue-chip stocks and bonds.

Municipal bonds: If interest rates get high enough Chip would be wise to lock in some medium to long-term tax-free bonds. In 1981 good quality municipals reached yields of 12 percent (free from both federal and state tax for in-state residents). It's hard to believe that Chip would go too far wrong over the long run by spreading a million dollars over several municipal issues if rates were to reach even 9 percent again.

In the end, Chip will probably be better off if he continues to hustle: his go-for-it mentality won't suddenly shut off. But he might pick a new direction. Any nonprofit organization could certainly use someone like him not only as a benefactor but as a forceful contributor of time and ideas. Chip can keep doing what he does best—working real-estate deals—and still put some of his time and energy into a new project of public service, which will probably be more satisfying ultimately than showing off his wealth.

His challenge will be to channel his energy in ways that continue to stimulate him. He can enjoy the extra time with his family, and he can also enjoy turning to the question many Hustlers never answer: how to *use* his money rather than just make it.

Twelve

The Gambler

There's a bit of the gambler in all of us, the part that's felt the thrill of winning in Las Vegas or the stock market.

Why does the Gambler choose to take risks where others are cautious? As usual, the reason has to do with what money means to him. Cautious people tend to weight money with their need for security; the Gambler weights money with his appetite for adventure. Gambling can be a lot of fun, whether it's an afternoon at the races or an hour with your broker. For the non-gambler, the fear of losing, of getting nothing for something, makes gambling unpleasant. For the Gambler, the thrill of the play, the hope of winning, of getting something for nothing, makes the risk worthwhile.

If it's adventure the Gambler is after, why this sort of adventure? Why not skydiving or race car driving or illicit romance? Why does the Gambler risk even a penny of the money he has worked hard to earn? At some level, conscious or not, the Gambler is playing out his resentment about the power money has over him. Just as the skydiver during free fall exults in his defiance of death, so the Gambler delights in his imprudence. "Do you think I respect your boring accountant-like rules?" he says to money. "Day in, day out, I'm your slave—counting you, saving you, protecting you.

Well, tonight in the casino, I say the hell with all that. With the help of Lady Luck, I'll bring you down."

We all harbor a secret hope that we'll be the ones to beat the odds. The Gambler is more willing than most to test that hope, to put all his money in a chancy biotechnic stock instead of good old IBM. It isn't greed that motivates the Gambler. Greed is more calculating, not as playful. The Gambler's defiance is human folly in full display. It is also a measure of our power to ignore reality.

Win or lose, the fun of gambling comes from those magical moments of hope and defiance—while the ball is whirling around the wheel, while the horses are pounding down the backstretch, while the game is tied in the last quarter, while the closing stock price is still unknown.

Aggressive with his money, the Gambler wants to see it grow. He wants to *play* with it. He wants risk and adventure. It's the commodities market for him, not stodgy mutual funds. The Gambler's style is a heady way of dealing with money, and it can drive some people crazy; problems are likely when a Gambler marries or becomes involved with a non-gambler. Risk-takers usually infuriate people who think life is risky enough as it is. Why tempt fate? That's precisely the point, the Gambler responds. He likes to tempt fate, to let fate know it doesn't own his soul.

The Gambler's admittedly irrational agreement with money is not destructive in its mild form. If it doesn't get out of hand, the Gambler can have a lot of fun and perhaps make a profit. But a Gambler may have a deeper and more potentially destructive agreement: "If I take wild risks with you, you will cure the boredom and depression I feel. I can't do it on my own, so you will turn me into someone special." We often overlook, or simply don't recognize, the passivity of the person who loves action. Indeed, he is so passive he's putting his life into the hands of luck. His agreement with money reflects that.

To make this money style work and not become a habit to break, the rational Gambler operates within limits and learns to separate a considered risk from a desperate hope. If you're worried that you, or your spouse or a friend, may have a gambling problem, ask yourself how you feel after a big loss. The pathological gambler feels nothing. Like the alcoholic treating a hangover, he treats that nonfeeling with more gambling.

The Pathological Gambler

It's a long way from gambling to pathological gambling. It's not merely a difference of degree but of kind. The pathological gambler is an addict, and risk is his drug. No matter how much he's won, he has to keep playing. It may be that he's addicted to losing, that what he's really after is the feeling that follows a big loss. He may be treating an underlying sense of guilt or the blah feeling of ordinary life.

Problem gambling isn't confined to seedy people or tacky casinos. Like problem drinking, it can affect anyone. Unfortunately, there is little public sympathy for this particular disability, so the syndrome often goes untreated until great financial and emotional damage has been done.

Why can't some people resist gambling? Why do some people turn that mild thrill into a habit as addictive, expensive, and dangerous as heroin? Pathological gamblers don't suffer from faulty consciences but from faulty nervous systems. Like alcoholics, they have a disease, not a moral infirmity. And as with alcoholism, there is no cure. There is, however, a means of control: total abstinence.

Like alcoholism, pathological gambling is likely a form of self-medication, a method of treating an underlying mood disorder such as chronic depression or manic-depressive illness. He feels an itch he can't scratch. He feels restless and bored to such an extraordinary extent that only reckless risk can treat it. He craves "action," which will disperse the restlessness and boredom as nothing else can. Just as the heroin addict becomes frantic in pursuit of his drug, so the pathological gambler will travel anywhere, sell, borrow, or steal anything, just to get his bet down. Once the bet is made, it's as if the drug has been injected. The high lasts until the result comes in. Afterward, win or lose, he must do it again. And again and again.

The pathological gambler doesn't need pep talks or sermons. Nor will it help to revile or exclude him. He needs not moral judgment but understanding and help, and he needs that desperately. Gamblers Anonymous and/or informed psychiatric intervention can be valuable.

The first goal of intervention is to provide supervision and support so that the gambling can be controlled. The next objective is to treat the underlying cause so that the crippling behavior won't return. It can be an arduous and frustrating process, but without it the lives of the pathological gambler and those close to him can be as tragic as those of any severe addict.

Making a Good Bet: Developing a Sound Financial Lifestyle

Rick is twenty-six years old, and since his graduation from Lehigh he has worked in sales for one of the nation's largest liquor manufacturers. His father owns a liquor store so Rick thought he'd go his dad one better and get into what he calls "corporate booze."

Rick's energetic personality has helped him advance rapidly. Including commissions and incentives, he made $42,000 last year and plans to top that this year. Living alone in a New Jersey condo, with a monthly mortgage payment of

$900 and traveling on business a lot, his expenses are low. He can live on his income comfortably, even with his occasional trips to Atlantic City. It doesn't hurt that his recently deceased grandfather left him $20,000.

Without a family—and with an appetite for risk—Rick figures this is his time to go for financial home runs. He wants to turn the $20,000 into $100,000 over the next five years. Rick is a rabid sports fan, and so far as he can tell the action of the stock market is similar to the thrill of the Knicks games he loves. He has a secret fantasy of making a "big killing" that would set him up for life. He worries, though, that this fantasy may be his greatest liability rather than a potential asset.

There is a rational approach to high-risk investing, and Rick is ideally situated for it. He genuinely enjoys risk-taking, and at this point in his life he can afford to lose it all, both financially and emotionally. He's a Gambler, but not a pathological gambler. He doesn't go crazy at the tables in Atlantic City: he has fun and feels excited, but stops before he's lost more than he would spend on a night on the town in Manhattan.

Where could he best invest his money to reach his $100,000 goal? Well, $20,000 will double in a little over seven years if it's put into a safe investment at 10 percent interest. Rick, though, wants to triple that performance, which means tripling the risk. Three common avenues are open if he's willing to explore them.

Stocks: Of particular appeal to people like Rick are the stocks of high-risk growth companies that sell over-the-counter. If one wants to increase both his risk and potential return by having more to invest he could buy stocks on margin, which means borrowing money from his broker, using his stock as collateral. If the stock drops too far in price in relation to the loan, though, the investor has to come up with extra cash or sell the stocks at a loss.

Options: Riskier than stocks, a stock option is a contract that, in theory, lets you buy a stock at a specific price for a specified period of time. You can win big. A 10 percent move (up or down) on a stock could mean a 50 percent move on one of the options for that stock, for example, if you guess right and your timing is good. The problem is that if the stock doesn't act the way you bet it would, you can lose all the money you paid for the option.

Futures: Even riskier than options, investing in futures involves highly leveraged betting (controlling far greater assets than actual cash invested) on the price movement of certain financial entities—the stock market, interest rates, gold, even pork bellies. But you can lose big, too, because you can't just walk away from your contract as you can with an option. You can end up owing the broker more money than you invested. Still, if you had invested in futures in early October 1987, betting that the stock market would go down, you would have made a fortune. (But do you know even one person who did?)

Whatever course he decides on, Rick should remember that no fail-safe system of playing the market has ever been invented, and no perfect stock market guru has ever been born.

Gambling Responsibly

Rick can enjoy the thrill of gambling—win or lose—but limit his risk by following a few rules:

Keep something in reserve. Rick already has his condo, a sound nonliquid investment. He should keep a few thousand in cash for the unforeseen emergency expense.

Pay mostly in cash. Granted, he's young and carefree. But Rick still shouldn't risk too much more than the money he has. He isn't rich. If he uses margin he shouldn't borrow the maximum.

Learn about stop and limit orders. That means specifying limits to your broker at which your stock will automatically be bought or sold. It's the equivalent of bringing only a fixed amount of money to the dice table and walking away when you've either run out of cash or reached a preset goal. Casino players, by the way, say that's the key to winning consistently at the gaming tables.

Hedge his bets. Brokers have a variety of ways of giving their customers what amounts to portfolio insurance. A common one is selling "call" options against stocks that you own. Rick could buy a stock because he thinks it will go up in price but sell options against it in case it doesn't. The same can be done in reverse.

Educate himself and get good advice. Blind investing may work in the short run if Rick is lucky, but in the long run he'll probably do better if he's well-informed. Rick should find a reliable broker and talk to him often. He should read the financial pages daily. In his own field, he might check out new small companies that look promising.

Control his impulses. Most gamblers have a problem with impulse control. Rick should beware of that impulse to buy a stock on some rumor or tip. One impulse buy can wipe out a year's gains.

Watch out! Does such "rational gambling" sound like it's taking the fun out of investing? Rick could put aside a small amount to blow on impulse bets if he wants to (either in Atlantic City or in the options market), but he should beware. The gambler's great defense, like the alcoholic's, is denial, and Rick's "small amount" could balloon into large debt if he doesn't watch it.

Thirteen

The Pessimist

There is a genus of sports fan that defines the Pessimist. It is a genus located largely in the Northeast, but there are outposts all over the world. It is called the Red Sox fan. The Red Sox have not won a World Series since 1918; yet they often come close, close enough to spark hope. But the minute a Red Sox fan feels hope sparked, he tells himself no, that cannot be. So begins the cycle. Consciously, he has long, often-repeated conversations with himself daily about why the team can't win. At the same time, deeper within him, in a pure and innocent part of his heart, hope is rising. At some point, usually in September, sometimes in August, rarely in October (it is a day more variable than Easter, but equally certain to come), hope and skepticism collide, and hope dolefully retreats amid derisive catcalls.

Some say the Red Sox will never win the World Series because Fenway Park is too small, or the left field wall is too high, or because the management is racist and will not sign the best black and Latin players, or because the team lacks speed, or because the atmosphere is too country club, or because the owners are too poor and George Steinbrenner is too rich, or because the team has always lacked a killer instinct, or because God wills it. None of these reasons, however plausible, is true.

The real reason the Red Sox will never win the World Series is that the Red Sox fans do not want them to. Why did the team trade Babe Ruth? Why did Johnny Pesky hold the ball? Why did Darrell Johnson pinch-hit for Jim Willoughby? Why did the ball go through Bill Buckner's legs? Because, quite simply, the fans wanted it. The fans so fill the team with their own gloom that the team can never win. And the fans' worldview remains intact.

So it is with the Pessimist and money. No matter how positive the outcome, there will always be bad news. Even as hope leads him to invest, reason will find a downside. No matter how good things seem, or how much money is simply rolling in, the Pessimist will fretfully look both ways as he crosses the one-way street. Ever a champion of Murphy's Law, after the last thing that can go wrong has gone wrong, he starts looking for the things that can't go wrong to go wrong.

When the Pessimist gets a raise he wonders if the company can afford to pay it. When the value of his house rises he worries that it's artificially inflated. If he wins a little in the lottery he worries about having used up his supply of good luck when he should have saved it for when he really needed it. When his dental bill is less than he thought it would be he wonders if the dentist forgot to fill a cavity.

Consciously, the Pessimist tells money, "I'm willing to work as hard for you as the next person, but come what may, you will let me down." His consistent expectation of the worst conceals an unconscious agreement with money that says, "If I doubt you persistently you will be true to me." The Pessimist believes he purchases pleasure with pain.

According to this superstitious agreement, it's bad luck ever to proclaim that things will be okay, that the money will be there. So the Pessimist continues to mutter gloom and doom, like magic imprecations over the cauldron of money, secretly making a bargain with money that it will reward his doubts with riches. Of course, the Pessimist, like the Red Sox fan, knows that by never letting himself hope, he may let many good opportunities pass him by.

Turning the Downside Up: Developing a Sound Financial Lifestyle

Hank Moore is a fifty-seven-year-old widower whose wife died fifteen years ago. A systems engineer for the Pentagon for the last three decades, Hank makes $50,000 a year and lives outside Washington, D.C. He has two married children, whom he put through college on the proceeds of his wife's life insurance.

A careful spender, by his fifty-fifth birthday Hank had managed to save $175,000, which he kept in a money market account. With a pension of $30,000 a year certain after retirement, he felt pretty secure. In late 1986, however, a friend of his who had doubled his own investments in the last year convinced Hank to get into the stock market.

Hank put $75,000 into solid blue-chip stocks, and by August 1987 his stake had grown to $105,000. Hank kicked himself for not getting in earlier. To make up for lost time, he put in another $25,000, this time in more speculative stocks. By the end of October, after the great crash, his $100,000 of invested capital was down to $65,000.

Enraged, Hank took out all his money and vowed never to invest again. He became convinced that the economy was headed for a recession. He put his house on the market, thinking real-estate values would soon dip, too, and got his asking price of $250,000. He bought a small condominium for $150,000. That left him with the following liquid assets:

Original savings not invested	$ 75,000
Stocks sold	65,000
Net from sale of house	100,000
Total Cash	$240,000

Hank has to decide what to do with his cash, all of which is back in his money market account. Although his money is safe where it is, he can probably get a higher rate of return while still taking little risk and keeping his money liquid. He would love a higher rate of return, but he's completely confused by and distrustful of all the financial ads in the papers. Brokers, banks, mutual funds, and insurance companies are always boasting about fantastic rates with seemingly little risk. But Hank thinks there has to be a catch (and there usually is).

There are lots of Hanks in the world. Most of us are pessimistic after taking a financial loss. There are, though, places where Hank could store his cash that really are very safe and that allow him to get his money out if he needs it. Here are a few of them:

Out-of-state bank money market funds: Hank may be able to get a higher interest rate on his funds just by using a different bank. *Money* magazine and *U.S.A. Today* often list high-yielding money fund rates of federally insured banks and S&Ls around the country.

Put bonds: These are bonds—municipal or corporate—that can be sold back to ("put" to) the issuer at face value on a specific date (or sometimes annually on a specific date until maturity). The put feature reduces the bond's yield but also reduces its price volatility because everyone knows that the issuer must buy the bond back at par on a certain date. There have been some excellent new issues recently with high tax-free yields and six-month put features.

Certificates of deposit: CDs range in maturity from thirty days to ten years, but shorter-term CDs are most appropriate for Hank. There are three places where he can buy them: directly from the banks and S&Ls that issue them, through stockbrokers, and through CD brokers. The CDs that stockbrokers sell can be traded on the open market before maturity for whatever the going value is at the time—much like a bond or Treasury note. The CDs that CD brokers offer generally have the highest yields because they are for troubled institutions that must pay a higher yield to attract deposits. Some experts feel that these CDs are a real bargain because they often pay 1 percent more than other CDs and yet are backed by the same federal insurance as the safest banks in the country. Whichever CD Hank chooses, he should be sure it has either FDIC or FSLIC insurance.

Variable-rate demand obligations: VRDOs are high-quality (usually AAA-rated) tax-free bonds that change their interest rate weekly and therefore always sell at par value (no price fluctuation). They are backed by major banks and pay an interest rate that is usually much higher than their closest competition: tax-free money market funds. There are two small drawbacks: they usually trade in $100,000 increments, and brokers are not very familiar with them (because they are paid almost nothing for selling them).

Each of the above instruments carries very little risk, has little or no transaction charge, and can be liquidated easily. There are many other investments that appear to be very safe and liquid that are heavily advertised in the financial pages, especially during bad economic times when people are looking for safety and income: unit trusts, bond mutual funds, Ginnie Maes, income-producing limited partnerships, government income funds, floating rate notes, and so on. While any of these instruments may turn out to be a good long-term investment (particularly during periods of declining interest rates), none of them in any way substitutes for a money market fund or is equal in safety to the four described above. None of them would be appropriate for Hank, for example, given his pessimistic outlook and recent market experience. Each has transaction costs and the possibility of substantial price fluctuation.

Expert Advice

The array of investment choices today is mind-boggling, and there is no shortage of financial gurus around to help people like Hank sort out these choices—for a price. But trying to figure out what all the experts have to offer and what this enlightenment will really cost you sometimes makes the situation even more confusing.

Everyone has a slightly different approach to handling money and a different opinion about what will work best. That's what makes a market. Even the people who you'd think should know contradict one another all the time. (Notice the difference in predictions often cited on Louis Rukeyser's popular *Wall Street Week* by any two experts. Each is articulate, experienced, and credible. Yet one of them, the pessimist knows well, is dead wrong.) More than in any other profession, the investment professional stands exposed to being proved wrong. While it is virtually impossible that a layperson could diagnose a heart problem, for example, more accurately than an experienced cardiologist, the novice investor can sometimes outsmart a top portfolio manager, broker, or securities analyst on any particular call.

So are there really any investment experts at all? Or is Hank right in thinking they are all overpaid promoters who can't really beat the odds any better than you can? Well, salesmanship is the backbone of Wall Street. And the majority of investment advertising, research reports, newsletters (and, yes, books) are not worth the paper they're printed on.

It's not that all financial advisers are dumb. Many are very intelligent and conscientious. The problem lies in the possibility that even the genuine expert may not be able to outwit the hand of fate in the long run. Supporting this notion is the sad fact that fewer than 40 percent of all professional portfolio managers—those handling mutual funds, pension funds, bank trust departments, and endowments—even beat the Standard & Poor 500 Index (considered the *average* performance) when it comes to playing the stock market.

Business school professors explain this phenomenon with their efficient market theory: with today's instant information and fierce competition, stock prices normally represent an accurate compendium of all that is known about the underlying companies. Over the long run, the theory holds, it is unlikely that investors will beat the market averages, especially when you figure in the disadvantage they have of management and transaction fees.

One professor begins his portfolio management course each year by calling the entire class of about sixty students to the front of the lecture hall, where he hands each of them a penny. He then asks his students to flip their coins simultaneously, trying as hard as they can to flip heads. After each slow and ceremonious round of flips ("Really concentrate this time," begs the professor), all unsuccessful students— the tails flippers—must turn in their pennies and take their seats. Eventually, after a dozen or so rounds, only one heads flipper remains, standing triumphantly in front of the class. "This unbelievably talented young man [or woman] will be our portfolio manager," the professor announces to thunderous applause. "This person's record gives us the best chance of beating the odds in the future."

Wall Street people hate stories like this. The entire investment industry is based on the theory that hard work and intelligent research can produce better results. Fortunately for the industry, most investors also believe that the odds can be beaten. It's almost un-American to accept a theory that says you can probably be only average in the long run. There just has to be a way that you can buy better odds. But Hank thinks he knows better.

A Simple Alternative to the Stock Market

Hank is not the first person to find beating the market a difficult game. And the market's return itself is not always spectacular. The average annual rate of return on stocks since World War II (measured by the Standard & Poor 500 Index), including both price appreciation and dividend income, comes to little more than 9 percent. And that doesn't take into consideration the cost of buying or selling.

There is, of course, no guarantee that one can get even 9 percent or any other specific return on equity investments. In order to have achieved the average return, Hank would have to have withstood tremendous variations in year-by-year returns and, as October 1987 clearly demonstrated, to have taken considerable risk of capital.

But what if he could get a *guaranteed* return that's as good as or better than the historical rate for high-risk investments such as stocks? And what if he could do that without paying any fees, with retaining total liquidity, and with the potential for an even higher rate of return than the stated guaranteed rate?

If interest rates are high enough—let's say 10 percent or above—*government-guaranteed zero coupon bonds* are an attractive and simple investment alternative for investors who don't want to take the risk, incur the fees, or bother with the complexities and uncertainties of the stock market or other equity investments. Instead of paying out interest every six months, the way regular bonds do, zeros are bought at a discounted price and grow at a certain rate of return until they mature. They are the most streamlined of all investments: there are no commissions, built-in management fees, withdrawal penalties, prospectuses to read, papers to sign, etc. All you get is a competitive yield and a full repayment promise on a specific date from the U.S. government. (Stocks, remember, go to infinity. There is no repayment promise on any date.) Zero coupons are especially attractive for retirement accounts, where the appreciation is also fully protected from tax.

Hank could buy a $100,000 face value (value at maturity date) government-guaranteed zero coupon bond, for example, for $50,000. At a rate of 10 percent, it would take a little more than seven years for the $50,000 to double in value to the $100,000. In the meantime, the bond could be sold at any point along the way for its market value at the time.

Is 10 percent a good enough rate to lock in for seven years? On the basis of historical data, it's fantastic. Yes, we all remember 1981, when rates on seven-year Treasuries were over 12 percent. But the average yield on seven-year Treasuries since World War II has been less than 6½ percent. And since there's no way in the world for Hank to figure out which way interest rates will go, he just shouldn't worry about it once he's locked in a historically attractive rate. If rates go up after he commits, he can just hold on. They'll come back down. And if they don't, the very worst that will happen is that he will get a 10 percent annual return on his hard-earned money for seven years while taking no risk and incurring no fees. He'll probably still beat most other investors. And if interest rates *decline* during his holding period, he'll have the opportunity to capture an even greater return on his money than the original 10 percent by selling before maturity. The chart below shows how this works.

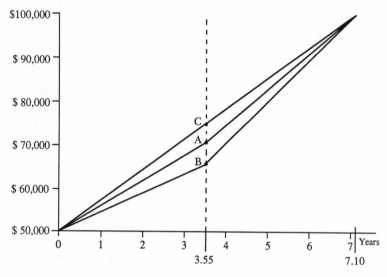

MID-LIFE OF A ZERO COUPON

Let's say Hank buys a $100,000 zero coupon Treasury that pays 10 percent for 7.1 years. He puts up $50,000 and is guaranteed $100,000 at maturity. Here's what his investment could look like at its halfway point, in 3.55 years. (Nothing particular happens halfway through, incidentally. We could come up with price scenarios at any other point just as easily.)

1. *Interest rates are the same.* Interest rates on competing instruments (3½-year Treasuries) are now exactly what they were on 7.1-year Treasuries when he started: 10 percent. What a coincidence! His $50,000 has compounded at 10 percent for the past 3½ years and is now worth exactly $70,711 (A) on the open market, in case he wants to sell it. If he keeps it until maturity instead, his $70,711 will continue to grow at 10 percent per year for another 3½ years until it reaches $100,000.

127

2. *Interest rates have gone up.* Uh-oh! Competing instruments are now yielding 12 percent, and Hank's stuck in a lowly 10 percent instrument. His broker says it's worth only $66,106 (B) if he wants to sell it, instead of the $70,711 theoretical midpoint value. He shouldn't panic. His investment is still worth 32 percent more than when he started. He can just hold on until interest rates come back down. The very worst he'll do is double his money and earn the original 10 percent per year over the full 7.1 years.

3. *Interest rates have come down.* Great! Competing instruments (3¹/₂-year Treasuries) are now yielding only 8 percent while Hank was smart enough to lock in 10 percent when rates were higher. Instead of being worth $70,711 at its halfway point, his security is now worth $75,684 (C). If he wants to, he can take his money and run. On the basis of this premium price, his investment has returned a whopping 12 percent per year for the first 3¹/₂ years.

Two notes on interest rates. First, the 10 percent (or whatever rate Hank locks in at time of purchase) will probably be neither the high nor the low point of the interest rate range during the next seven years. It would be quite a coincidence if it were. The important thing is that he starts out with a guaranteed rate that is historically high and that historically beats other types of investment over time. If he wants to bet on exact interest rates, he can go back to the stock market.

Secondly, shorter-term instruments normally yield less than longer-term instruments. Thus, a 3¹/₂-year Treasury bond would be expected to yield less than a 7-year Treasury bond, putting the zero coupon investor at a distinct advantage as time passes because his original rate is competing against shorter- and shorter-term maturities.

If Hank is right and we're headed for very bad times, he may have been wise to move to a smaller place; he might have done even better to rent. In times of rampant inflation, as in the 1970s, real estate is a great investment; during prolonged deflation, real estate is not the place to be.

Hank also might consider putting a fraction of his money—5 percent—into gold. Gold is basically a high-risk investment—it has fluctuated hundreds of dollars an ounce in the past ten years—but as the traditional money standard it's a sound investment to have in case of a total economic collapse. The price fluctuation, lack of income, and expense of buying, storage, and insurance are negative factors, but a small amount may make a Pessimist like Hank feel more secure.

On a day-to-day basis, Hank will feel most comfortable spending as little as possible, avoiding major purchases like a new car or an expensive vacation. If he accumulates cash and keeps it in safe, liquid accounts, he can protect himself while he waits to see what shape the bad times will take. And if he's wrong, he'll be prepared for good times as well.

Fourteen

The Miser

To the Miser, money is control, and control is crucial. Parting with money means parting with a bit of his grip on reality. He hoards his money in the conscious hope that he'll have enough when he needs it, and in the unconscious hope that he will live forever. He is stockpiling against fate.

To the Miser, spending money is like showing emotion: both are unacceptable threats to his psychic integrity. He is usually as withholding of his feelings as he is of his money. Unlike Ebenezer Scrooge, unfortunately most Misers don't undergo the transformative process of being visited by ghosts. Rather, they are pestered by chronic, unrealistic fantasies of poverty that render them unable to let go of a penny without feeling pain.

Misers may be rich or poor. It is a commonplace observation, and a true one, that some of the richest people are peculiarly stingy. Indeed, wealthy people can become almost fanatical in their attention to nickels and dimes. This may be a way of avoiding coming to terms with the enormity of their fortunes. They pretend instead that they have little, and their only control is to hold onto every cent. Or it may be that miserliness is the way they got rich in the first place: take, don't give, and hold on to it all.

The Miser is normally guarded; he reveals nothing about

his finances, not even to his own family, who are amazed when he dies and the will is read. Sometimes he is far, far wealthier than anyone imagined. He acts as if keeping his finances secret is vital to national security. In fact, it is vital to his own security. Emotionally, he has made the connection between financial secrecy and salvation. To reveal anything is to risk losing everything. Because money can corrupt everyone, the only safety is to tell nothing to anyone. Always keep your guard up. Never trust.

Advising such a person is virtually impossible. For one thing, he won't reveal enough to make any advice meaningful. And he won't trust any advice anyway. About the only way to affect a person like this is to agree with him, or to go him one better. Tell him the world is even more dangerous than he thinks it is. Tell him that if anything he's too trusting. He'll either realize you're kidding and perhaps laugh at himself or, more likely, think you're shrewd.

Obviously, this isn't a convivial money style, nor a style that wins friends, although it usually does influence people. The Miser tends to be lonely, keeping company with his gold and his gruesome fantasies. Along the way he usually alienates many people—family, friends, business associates. As he rejects, he is rejected, but rather than changing, he becomes increasingly bitter and resolute. Over time, money becomes not only the symbol of his control but the substance of his love. His holdings become his paramour.

Another kind of miser is more common than the traditional Scrooge. This is the person who is miserly only with himself. He will give to others, often being quite generous, but when it comes to spending on himself he can't do it. Often a religious person for whom self-gratification borders on sin, this congenial Miser can spend on others because it's a form of giving, sanctioned by his moral code. But spending on himself is too guilt-provoking to be enjoyable.

It can be argued that the 1980s could have used a hefty

dose of such self-miserliness and that we would all benefit from spending less on ourselves. But at times, such self-denial can approach a sort of martyrdom that frustrates and worries other people. Although in the long run it may be better to give than to receive, psychologically speaking it can be just as important, and just as generous, to be able to receive as well as to give.

Family or friends may feel exasperated at the Miser's routine of self-denial, wishing happier conditions for him. Or they may feel guilty about their own spending while poor old Mom or Dad makes such extreme sacrifices. When money becomes so tinged with the guilt of self-indulgence that it can't be spent, the pain this causes for others can be acute.

Not everybody who spends very little is a Miser. Some people are simply very inventive and imaginative around money, able to make a little go a long way. They don't buy a table; they find a beautiful old door at a junkyard and make their own. They don't buy designer names; they design themselves. These aren't the people we're addressing. It's not the amount spent (or not spent) that makes one a miser; it's the emotions involved.

Loosening the Money Belt: Developing a Sound Financial Lifestyle

Mary Flaherty, seventy-four years old and a widow, lives alone in Naples, Florida. When her husband died ten years ago, she sold their house in New Jersey for $450,000 and fled the cold winters for Florida, where she paid cash for a $100,000 condominium.

A woman who came of age during the Depression, Mary never got over feeling poor. Although she is generous with her children and grandchildren, she's a miser with herself.

She draws her bath only three inches full to save water. She strains to read by low-wattage bulbs. She cuts out coupons in the newspaper every day and walks across town to buy hamburger on sale. (She likes to walk, but she also likes to save on gas.) She exasperates her children by taking the bus to visit them in New Jersey instead of paying for a plane ticket.

Mary lavishes presents on her eight grandchildren, and recently paid off $30,000 in consumer debts one of her sons had run up. She goes to church every day and gladly puts $5 in the collection plate. But she's worn the same raincoat for ten years, and the car her kids insisted she buy goes largely unused.

In fact, Mary is well off. In addition to the $350,000 she netted when she changed houses, she also received $200,000 in life insurance, plus she gets Social Security and a pension. Her yearly income is nearly $85,000, $60,000 after taxes.

Last year Mary spent $14,000 on herself; the rest went to her church, charities, and family. She seems to be aware that she has money for others, but she can't comprehend her fortune applying to herself. (Some years she does manage to save some of her money.)

John, her son and financial adviser, has invested most of her money in stocks, bonds, and mutual funds at a brokerage house. The only part of her monthly statement she reads is the few dollars she spends on the debit card they gave her. The rest of the statement has too many columns for her to bother with. In the crash of 1987, when she lost about $75,000, she didn't even notice it. She simply deposits her monthly checks and spends as little as she humanly can in order to stay within her tight budget.

Mary is an active and vigorous woman; she loves walking, swimming, playing bridge, and entertaining her friends. But she drives her children crazy with her constant poor-mouthing. "I'd take the bridge cruise if it weren't so pricey." "A new coat is out of the question." Her catalog of the things she'd like to do if she could afford them is endless.

Selective miserliness like this isn't uncommon among people who went through the Depression. The first question for Mary and her children is to figure out whether or not she actually does have any financial problems. Although she claims there are things she'd like to do, Mary's fear and guilt over spending on herself may be too great for her ever to enjoy it. Her children may just have to accept that she is happy as she is. But there are a few things Mary and her family might try to do.

Talk dollars and sense. John could sit down with her and show her how little money she saves by shivering in three inches of bathwater or by burning a 40-watt bulb instead of a 100. He might try to educate her about the larger picture—what it means to have over half a million dollars at her age. Of course, he has to be careful: if the amount she lost in the market ever sinks in, she might never invest a cent again. John might begin by writing out a simple balance sheet for her, like the ones on pages 94 and 103.

Ease into change gently. Mary might try an experiment, making a deal with her family. Once a week she might do something nice for herself that costs money she doesn't usually spend. And once a month she might do something especially nice, like take the bridge cruise. At the end of eight months or so, if she isn't enjoying her new way of life, her family will agree to accept Mary as a dyed-in-the-wool miser and tolerate her complaining. If the experiment succeeds, both Mary and her family can enjoy her pleasure.

Consult her peers. If Mary talked more with her friends about how they enjoy their money, that might help her to break down her resistance. It might also help to talk to her priest; some of her self-denial may be rooted in her religion.

Find better ways to save. Getting good tax advice might

uncover ways of saving money on the gifts Mary gives that far exceed her habitual petty economies. That might provide the underpinnings of a rationale for spending a bit more on herself. Taxes are by far her greatest expense. Her son John might make another deal with her: whatever he can save her in taxes, she will spend on frivolities for herself she now thinks she can't afford.

Tax Advice—Good, Bad, and Indifferent

If you ask most people what their greatest expense in life is, odds are you'll get an earful about mortgage payments or the soaring cost of tuitions. But those answers are almost always wrong. *Taxes* are by far the greatest expense most of us will ever endure. Despite recent reductions in personal income tax rates, the average American still works until May 5th each year to pay his taxes.

Despite the epidemic of tax cheating and the mass paranoia that visits America every April 15, serious tax planning throughout the year is practiced by few. It's probably safe to say that most people aren't even sure which bracket they are in (even though there are now only three brackets).

Mary is very typical of someone who pays almost no attention whatsoever to her taxes, and, as a result, probably pays more than she has to. How do taxes affect her investments and other aspects of her financial life? Let's say that someone in her situation were paying a 33 percent federal tax and 7 percent state tax (although in Florida he or she wouldn't be) on at least some of his or her income this year. Here are just a few examples of how taxes could influence that person's overall financial planning:

—His 6 percent money market fund is really paying him only about 3½ percent after taxes.

135

—That 9 percent in-state municipal bond her broker called about is the equivalent of earning 15 percent on a taxable bond.

—That $8,000 bonus he's hoping for this year is worth only $4,800 after taxes.

—That $600 she saved on her airline tickets by planning ahead is the same as having earned an extra $1,000 of taxable income.

Tax Shelters

What about tax shelters? You can't evade paying taxes, but you can avoid being taxed. One is considered fraud; the other is considered smart financial planning.

Just about anything can be (and probably has been) construed as a tax shelter, but the original intent of Congress in giving tax incentives was to encourage capital investment in certain areas (or to reward certain interest groups) that it felt were particularly worthy, such as low-income housing, energy exploration, or research and development.

Most people are green with envy when they hear about some tax-sheltering scheme they missed out on, but they shouldn't be. Many tax-shelter investments, past and present, are terrible deals in which only the promoter will ever make a cent, while the unlucky investors will always regret the day they met him.

A good tax adviser will tell you that it's often better just to pay your taxes—even at a 30 to 40 percent total rate—than to complicate your life with questionable tax or investment schemes. There is no legal means of making taxes just go away. Tax sheltering basically means *deferring* tax into future years (although it also used to include converting income into long-term capital gains, as well as getting tax credits for certain investments). The tax is still owed, to be "recaptured" by Uncle Sam in the future, although paying later is the equivalent of an interest-free loan from the government.

But nowadays, if you defer enough you may get hit with an extra "alternative minimum tax" in the meantime. Even worse, some tax-shelter investors can owe so much in future taxes they're actually bankrupt and don't even know it.

The world of taxes is very complicated. So where do you get advice? There are basically three ways to handle your taxes: do them yourself, go to a "commercial" tax preparer, or use a tax professional.

Do It Yourself

Most people still do their taxes themselves. There are many helpful books explaining the new tax code and how to prepare your return. They range from J. K. Lasser's perennial best-seller to publications put out by the IRS itself. They all have samples of every IRS form and explain how each is to be filled out. The non-government ones have lists of reminders and helpful ideas on how to take full advantage of each rule. Some even explain the great mystery of what exactly happens to your return after it is filed (Does somebody actually read these things?) and why some returns are audited.

You can also do your taxes on your home computer. There are many programs to choose from now that make tax calculations a lot less tedious, once you get used to them. With a good tax program, instructions are clearer, IRS forms appear instantly, and recalculations are done automatically. Prices for tax software range from about $50 to $250, depending on what the program does and how many schedules it includes. Make sure the program you choose has all the forms that your taxes require, and find out how much on-screen help it gives you when you're stuck.

Commercial Preparers

This is the easiest method; it's also the one in which the taxpayer gets the least involved. Depending on how you feel about your money, you may find this kind of help attractive. But it's usually not the best idea.

H&R Block is a good example because it's the biggest and best known. It has thousands of January-through-April offices all over the country in which some 50,000 seasonal preparers crank out tax returns on commission. (The preparers have had approximately three weeks of basic tax training.) Their average fee is about $50 for a federal and state return with itemized deductions.

This kind of basic service is all right for taxpayers whose financial lives are not particularly complex (Block clients average $35,000 in annual income) and who otherwise would not spend the time required to do their own tax planning or the money required to get expert help. But as you can imagine, what you don't get here is the personal and creative year-round service that's necessary if you are in a higher income bracket and are serious about really saving money on taxes.

Professional Help

If you do take tax planning seriously, have a fairly complex financial life, and don't have the time or inclination to struggle with it yourself, then find yourself a good tax professional.

In some states, where there's no licensing procedure, anyone can call himself an accountant. So the title "public accountant" doesn't tell you much about the person's training. An "enrolled agent" is an accountant who has passed certain IRS requirements. And a CPA (certified public accountant) has passed an even more stringent series of examinations. Enrolled agents and CPAs may represent their clients at IRS audits and appeals, while public accountants and commercial tax preparers may not. If you are going to rely on someone else for tax advice, you may as well increase your chances of competent help by getting a CPA.

There are many ways in which a creative CPA can help you save some money on taxes: reviewing retirement plans, helping you keep better records of expense items, recommending tax swaps of securities to reduce capital gains, estate planning, setting up trusts for children, or deferring income or gains to more advantageous tax years (very important between 1986 and 1988 as tax rates declined).

Even after spending the money it takes to get top-notch tax advice, unfortunately you can't simply turn over this part of your financial life to someone else and forget about it. The more information you can give your CPA, the more he will be able to help you. But don't expect him to know everything. Questions of tax law, for example, are usually more reliably answered by tax lawyers than CPAs. And a tax adviser won't necessarily know anything about investments, although people are always asking their accountant and lawyer for investment advice because they deal with related aspects of the financial world.

The cost of tax advice is surprisingly high—up to $200 an hour—and you can't imagine how they come up with all those hours. But spending a few thousand dollars a year on someone very creative could save you many times that amount in taxes.

Fifteen

The Worrier

Everyone worries about money. It's only logical—we depend on it for so much. We all have different styles of worrying: some of us worry about money a little each day; others once a month in a general anxiety attack when we pay our bills. Some of us hand over the worry to someone else, such as a spouse or a financial manager. Some of us deal with the worry paradoxically, by overspending, while others try never to spend at all. Some of us deal with the worry by trying to deny that it exists; others, like accountants, master it by making it their line of work. But there is also the person who worries excessively, extremely, almost nonstop.

This perpetual state of anxiety resembles the state of mind of people who are obsessed with their weight. Should I have a martini, or wine, which is less fattening, or a Perrier? Can I have dessert if I eat nothing tomorrow? I should weigh myself before I have lunch.

The money Worrier is similarly obsessed, not only by the big worries but also by daily little mosquito-bite worries. Will the check clear on time? Did I pay too much for that dress? What if the automatic teller machine forgot to record my deposit? Do I really have to tip the waiter 15 percent even though the service was poor? Am I a petty person for feeling jealous of my friend who got a raise, even though I know she deserved it? Why didn't I buy that stock yesterday?

Many of you can identify with those examples, but you're a true Worrier only if concerns like these make up the great part of your day, if money is at once a terrifying subject and one you can't leave alone. For the true Worrier, worry is infused into every process involving money. Money neither comes in nor goes out without being worried about. There is no such thing as an easily written check or a casually made deposit. Small purchases require rumination before they're made and afterward. Large transactions, such as buying a house or a car, lead almost to hospitalization before they can be completed. A windfall may lead to a fainting spell; an audit from the IRS can be lethal.

The Worrier's anxiety about money often stems from the displacement of other, nonfinancial worries. This doesn't happen consciously, of course. The Worrier doesn't say, "I'm too nervous to deal with my concerns about love, power, security, and self-esteem, so I'll divert them all onto money and just worry about that." But the fact is that as unpleasant as it is to worry all the time about money, it's more comfortable than worrying about those other things.

There are other causes of the Worrier's anxiety. Money may be used to reenact other, earlier worries. A child who grows up in an insecure environment of parents' divorcing, remarrying, moving, drinking, may reenact those childhood feelings of insecurity and lack of trust in adulthood through the medium of money, which provides the most available daily stage on which to act out that drama.

The true Worrier needs help—if not counseling, then sustained conversations with a friend or a spouse. The goal is to discover and deal with the underlying causes for the extreme and disabling worry. As for the average worrier, the best advice for dealing with worry is simple—never worry alone. Tell your spouse, your lawyer, your accountant, your financial manager. The likelihood is that they will be able to reassure you. Worrying alone about money, like worrying alone about anything else, intensifies the worry and magnifies the problem. The average worrier can become the Worrier.

Worrying Well: Developing a Sound Financial Lifestyle

Libby Prescott is a twenty-five-year-old social worker who lives in Cleveland. Growing up on a small farm in Ohio, she acquired her parents' warmth as well as their tendency toward financial worry. After graduation from Ohio State, she decided on social work, which she loved, even though she knew the pay was woefully low. Now, though, she has nightmares about money. Not a day passes without guilt about some money spent or dread about some impending expense. She obsesses constantly about whether to switch to a higher-paying career in order to avoid a life of scrimping.

Libby lives with another single woman in a rented apartment and feels guilty that she resents having to do so. She drives a used Datsun and lives in terror of the water pump breaking as it did last December. She has to dress reasonably well for work, and although she makes as many of her clothes as she can and spends very little, she still agonizes over her clothes budget. She loves the one good vacation she takes a year, but she worries about that, too. Frugal by nature, Libby contributes the maximum amount to her IRA, but she worries that something will go wrong with the economy and the money will disappear before she gets it. Her only other savings is a mutual fund her parents bought for $250 when she was born, which is now worth about $2000.

The best way to help a Worrier is to hold up his or her worries against the light of reality. Libby's salary is $25,000 a year; these are her monthly expenses:

Rent	$	300
Car and insurance		233
Clothes		150
Food		200
Taxes		416
IRA		166
Vacation and travel		166
Telephone and utilities		50
Miscellaneous spending		400
Total		$ 2,081 a month
		$24,972 a year

Libby is as well or better off than most people her age. She has no dependents, good job security, and excellent benefits. She isn't living in a terribly expensive city. Assuming Libby wants to be a social worker, she's off to a good start.

The IRA

Her financial future doesn't look that bad either. Although she shouldn't rely on it, Libby will probably marry and be at least somewhat better off on a combined income. Her IRA is a fine idea. Not only is it a tax deduction and a forced savings plan, but in the long run she could have a sizable nest egg to fall back on.

An IRA is at least a partial solution to two of life's greatest financial worries: taxes and retirement. IRAs allow anyone with earned income to set aside up to $2,000 a year ($4,000 total for a working couple or $2,250 total for one working and one with no income). If you have an IRA, you will eventually have to pay taxes on this money (as you withdraw it during retirement), but in the meantime you can (1) take a tax deduction each year (if you have no other retirement plan); (2) defer the tax on any income or gains you make in the account each year (this part applies to everyone); (3) force yourself to save money if you make automatic contri-

143

butions to your plan each month through your employer, bank, or broker.

A *Keogh plan* is like a giant IRA. Available only to self-employed people (or employees who also have self-employed income), it permits you to contribute up to 20 percent of your gross income (up to $30,000 each year). Keogh and IRA funds need not be invested only in savings accounts or CDs, although that's where most people have them. The funds may be placed in a wide variety of investments, including stocks, bonds, and mutual funds.

Worriers often worry less when they start doing something constructive to help themselves financially. There are ways Libby could increase her income, perhaps by moonlighting in an evening clinic or developing a small private practice. She might even get some training and try an entirely different field on weekends. A lot of people work part-time in real estate, for instance. The warmth and sincerity that work so well in social work could transfer here readily, and her commission on the sale of just a few houses a year could match her current income. In short, if Libby used the time and energy she spends on worrying to augment her income instead, she would worry less.

Libby also could find ways to cut her expenses—move into a larger apartment with more roommates, for example, or sell her car and use public transportation, cut back or cut out her vacation. But these efforts might be too demoralizing and might make her resent her job. Because she has demonstrated the ability to save with her IRA, she might think about building up some equity by making payments on a condominium as soon as her salary rises sufficiently.

Channeled properly, Libby's worrying can become a motivator rather than an inhibitor.

Sixteen

The Dodger

The Dodger knows that money matters. He simply can't or won't master the mechanics of managing it wisely. The very subject makes him intensely anxious. He wishes it would go away and leave him alone. His attitude is like the plea in court of nolo contendere: "Do whatever you want, Judge; I don't want to fight it." "Do what you will, Money; it's too much of a hassle to take you on."

The Dodger often is subject to one of the more common tricks money plays. Its mere mention turns the brain of an otherwise intelligent person to mush. Sudden in its onset, the phenomenon is extraordinary to behold. In the middle of a conversation with a friend, you ask in passing his opinion about a stock you're planning to buy. Eyes that were directed straight at you avert, hands that were calmly folded on the table turn to drumming fingers. The signal is clear: change the subject.

Dodgers often go to enormous lengths to avoid thinking about money. They aren't phobic about money; like most people, they usually enjoy it. But to think about money, really bring their intellect to bear on the subject, is out of the question. That prospect brings them to their cerebral knees. Instantly they feel inadequate. "I simply can't deal with these matters." "My accountant handles all of that." "I've never understood money." "I'm no good at math."

Typically, the Dodger works hard and earns a good living. People think he's in good financial shape. But his dirty little secret is that he has made no provision for the future, knows little or nothing about his mortgage, his life insurance, his investments, etc. He makes occasional halfhearted attempts to get advice, but soon gives up the effort. Every now and then his lack of planning leads to a small crisis—a bank balance way out of whack, lost investments, forgotten financial obligations. He beats himself over the head for his sin and resolves to do better, but basically he can't.

The Dodger is the underachiever of money styles. It isn't that he's above money or serenely indifferent to it. He *knows* it's important, and if you can get him to talk about it he will tell you earnestly that he wishes he were better at handling it. But two enormous obstacles stand in his way—boredom and anxiety.

There's nothing intrinsically interesting in most of the nuts and bolts of money management. It requires a methodical approach that's too tedious for many people. And the interesting parts—the decision-making, the risk-taking—can be scary.

Of course, every Dodger has his own reason for his dislike of dealing with money. It may have to do with a lack of training—parents who met every need, for instance. It may involve an unconscious association between money and greed or corruption. Reluctance and apparent indifference serve as a self-protective device for these people, who simply can't stand the anxiety money makes them feel. They could be much happier if they would stare down their money demons, master them, and then use common sense and information to make their plans.

The Dodger's attitude has nothing to do with intelligence. Indeed, he often is highly skilled in his own field. If he put his mind to it he probably could become an expert in finance, but the idea of doing that makes him ill. Rather, the phenomenon has to do with an emotional conflict over money. He craves money as a source of power, but at the same time feels guilty about that craving. So money becomes a source of conflict to be avoided. In its simplest form, the conflict is, "I want more/I can't get more." Rather than using intelligence and creativity to figure out ways of getting more, he tunes out.

The Dodger's agreement with money is: "I'll work to get you, but I won't work to take care of you. Short of disaster, I don't want to hear anything from you or know anything about you." For some Dodgers, the unconscious part of this agreement may be, "Financial success makes me feel nervous (or guilty). Therefore, I will avoid doing what I have to do to handle money." Because the Dodger does not appear to have any particularly crippling hang-ups related to money, other than a generalized anxious avoidance, he is probably the best able to be helped by a change in his habits.

Artful Dodging: Developing a Sound Financial Lifestyle

Karen Gardner is a forty-seven-year-old divorcée who lives in Minneapolis with her two teenage sons. A partner in a successful antiques business with three other women, Karen's contributions to the enterprise are her encyclopedic knowledge of the field and her engaging manner with customers. The business has done extremely well; it has even been written about in national magazines. Karen's partners agree she's the life of the shop, that it never would have succeeded without her.

While her partners' net worths have risen, however, Karen's has increased only moderately. She puts her draw— $40,000 last year—into her checking account, from which it disappears predictably. She doesn't live extravagantly, but paying taxes, rent (she hasn't got around to buying her home), and half her sons' private school tuition take a big bite out of her income. The additional $16,000 she receives in alimony and child support seems to evaporate too. At least Karen hasn't had to dig into her nest egg—part of her divorce settlement—of $75,000. She keeps this in a pass-book savings account. Here is how Karen spends her $56,000 income, broken down into an approximate monthly budget.

Taxes	$ 1,333
Rent	1,000
Tuition	416
Clothing	416
Food, including dinners out	583
Vacation, entertainment	416
Car expenses	250
Miscellaneous spending	250
Total	$ 4,664 a month
	$56,000 a year

People have no idea how close to the edge Karen lives; she usually puts it out of her own mind as well. She dresses well and carries herself with an air of confidence that gives no hint of financial insecurity. Her incisive remarks about an antique contrast strikingly with her inner bewilderment about what to do about money. She is determined to make sense of it . . . someday.

She keeps meaning to sit down with a financial planner. She knows that owning one-fourth of a successful business, plus an income of $56,000 a year, ought to put her in a better financial position. But she'd rather go on an antiques run to London, or even clean out her closets, than make money plans. Lately, with college looming for her sons,

Karen has begun to worry about money more, but she expects her former husband to come through.

Karen could be doing a lot better. For one thing, she's paying far too much in taxes. And since she's neither particularly strapped nor phobic about money, she's an ideal candidate for reaping the financial and emotional rewards that financial control would give her. Before Karen does anything related to the specifics of money management, though, she has to become involved with the feel of money, by getting on a first-name basis with it. Otherwise, whatever she does will probably be incomplete.

Karen can—and should—go at this gradually. She might begin by reading the *Wall Street Journal,* starting with the human interest stories, then reading whatever else catches her eye. A lot of money novices get hooked on the *Journal.* It's a dramatic recounting of the daily story of money, good at dispelling the boredom Karen feels when she thinks about the subject. As she progresses, Karen may want to try one of the investment guides available; one of the most helpful and enjoyable is Andrew Tobias's *The Only Other Investment Guide You'll Ever Need.*

Before she gets to that, though, she might plan to talk with her partner who handles the business finances, whose knack for money matches Karen's popularity with customers. Someone like this, who knows Karen, is ideally suited to help give her a feel for the topic, to help detoxify it, to show Karen that handling money competently is actually fun. If you're learning to ski, an able and sympathetic friend is the ideal person to take you from the scary beginner slopes to the top of Aspen. Money is no different.

Karen says she has been meaning to see a financial planner. Her first consultant, however, should be her business friend. If she goes to a broker or a financial planner too soon, she probably will conceal her ignorance and reluctance out of pride or anxiety. She will come across as confident and

149

self-assured (as she does in business) and agree to things she doesn't really understand.

As she begins to become more knowledgeable about money, Karen's reluctance will begin to fade and she will become more curious and confident. When she shops she will ask questions she considered too dumb before. She will learn to bargain in her personal life—say, in buying a car—as well as she does in business. At some point she will be able to sit down with an accountant who will help her ease her tax burden, perhaps by suggesting a retirement plan—an IRA, Keogh, or 401(K)—which will provide her with forced savings as well as a tax deduction. He probably will also suggest that she consider buying a home—another form of forced savings and another tax deduction, as well as much needed equity.

As her feel for the subject grows, Karen will be ready to start to invest some of her nest egg, at which point she will be able to make good use of a financial consultant. He should guide her to the low-risk investments that are right for her but that can provide greater growth and income than a savings account.

Depending on how well she takes to investing, she might end up putting her money in a passive investment such as a mutual fund. Who knows, though? A Dodger like Karen could get so involved in the process, she may find herself debating a variety of investment strategies with her broker. Karen doesn't have to become a financial wizard, of course. Antiques will probably always be her first love. But she can discover there is a humanist's entry into the world of money, and pleasure—not only financial—to be gained from being informed. Her standard of living may not rise substantially, but properly managed, her money can provide some future security for herself and some current added security as she discovers one more area of her life of which she's in control.

Since the passive world of mutual funds is often appealing to Dodgers, or reformed Dodgers, like Karen, it might be helpful to discuss the basic concepts of this investment vehicle.

A Mutual Fund Primer

The mutual fund concept is appealing for small investors who don't want to be involved with the monitoring and decision-making required by investing in individual securities. Funds have what many investors want: diversification, professional management, liquidity, automatic reinvestment of income and gains, and often good potential for growth. It's not hard to find out which funds have performed well and to monitor your own fund by referring to any of the numerous services and newsstand magazines that track them.

A mutual fund is simply a package of securities owned by a large group of investors and managed by a designated portfolio manager. The investors come and go, buying and redeeming shares at will. Shares of the fund represent partial ownership in the fund's entire portfolio, perhaps hundreds of different stocks or bonds. The value of the fund shares is determined not by supply and demand for the fund itself (as stock values are determined), but by the exact value of the securities in the fund. The fund manager has discretion to buy and sell securities as he chooses, so long as they fit the stated objectives of the fund.

There are over 2,000 registered mutual funds today. You can find one that specializes in almost any type of investment you're interested in: stocks, bonds, money market instruments, mortgages, foreign securities, convertible bonds, tax-free bonds, junk bonds, government securities, and many, many others. Wall Street quickly packages almost any investment craze. It is best to choose one that is congruent with your financial goals and the degree of risk you are willing to assume.

The following is a brief guide to some of the broad categories of mutual funds:

Growth funds look for capital appreciation, so they buy common stocks. The type of stocks a growth fund goes after could be almost anything—high-risk small companies, international stocks, companies within a particular industry, or any other means of producing capital appreciation. But the portfolio manager's goal is always to beat the competition: the money market rate, the various stock indexes, and, most importantly, other mutual funds.

Income funds buy bonds, preferred stocks, mortgage instruments, notes, or any other security that pays a high dividend or interest rate. Fixed income managers want not only to produce as much income as they can, but they must always be concerned with principal, because their market values are influenced greatly by the movement of interest rates. Income funds are mainly for people who need to spend the income (many are retirees), although dividends can be reinvested for people who don't.

Balanced funds are made up of a combination of income and growth securities. Their objective is to provide some income but also to achieve growth (capital appreciation) through their common stock investments. Many of these funds buy convertible securities.

Money market funds exploded in popularity in the early 1980s when interest rates went through the roof. Unlike all other mutual funds, they are always priced at $1.00 per share. They invest in highly secure (CDs, Treasury bills, commercial paper) and short-term instruments for the purpose of safety, income, and liquidity. Because there is no price fluctuation and the income is accrued daily, money market funds have become a combination savings and checking account for many people in recent years.

Sector funds are mutual funds that invest in several stocks of one specific industry. A drug sector fund, for example, might include shares of Bristol-Myers, Upjohn, Warner-Lambert, Merck, SmithKline, and so on.

Most large investment companies now offer a wide variety of funds within the same family of funds. Fidelity Group, the largest mutual fund company, now offers over one hundred individual funds, including many sector funds. An investor can switch easily from one fund to another with a toll-free phone call. And there's no shortage of switch-fund advisory letters to subscribe to. For a few hundred dollars a year, they will share their wisdom about market timing and tell you whether stocks, bonds, or cash look best to them at any given time. (But how many of them called for all cash prior to October 1987?)

The family-of-funds concept is a good approach for novice investors like Karen. If interest rates are on the rise and stocks and bonds are falling, you can keep your money safe and liquid in the group's money market fund. If rates start falling and you want to lock in a diversified portfolio of bonds, you can switch some of your money into that portfolio. And if you feel adventurous it may be time to switch some money into your fund's stock portfolio. You will usually have a choice of several different stock funds, each with a different style and objective. Sounds easy, doesn't it? Just buy low and sell high. The hard part is figuring out how low is low and how high is high.

How do you find the best performers? *Forbes, Business Week,* and *Money* magazines conduct extensive annual surveys on the performance of mutual funds. Beware of hot mutual funds being pushed by their sponsors. Every year some type of fund will perform spectacularly while last year's hot group is already in a downswing. The gold funds were hot in the late 1970s as the price of gold soared, but they fizzled out as the price of gold plummeted. Funds that specialize in other specific investment segments—energy, technology, and foreign stocks—have had similar cycles in recent years. Any fund can look good under certain market conditions. But consistency over a long period of time, through bad market conditions as well as favorable ones, is what the wise investor should look for. Check a fund's five- and ten-year record more carefully than its most recent one-year record.

Mutual funds are not perfect investments and, of course, they are not for everyone. Most funds, for example, would not be appropriate for very conservative investors because there is always some element of risk. On the other hand, a more aggressive investor who likes to get personally involved with specific investment decisions, would find a mutual fund too passive. Funds are usually best suited for passive investors like the Dodger, who want long-term capital growth or a long-term total return from a combination of income and growth.

Seventeen

The Victim

Unlike the Dodger, who avoids thinking about money, the Victim deals with money but in a way that always puts him on the losing end. To some extent, we are all victims of money. Most of us feel we never have enough. "Feel" is the operative word here, because if we think about it we can usually realize either that we do have enough or that we have structured our relationship with money so that we don't have enough. Rather than recognizing that we victimize ourselves, we feel that money victimizes us.

There's the bill that comes in at just the wrong time, or the insurance that suddenly skyrockets, the unexpected illness or the rise in tuition, the root canal, the bill for those presents we bought on vacation when we felt so devil-may-care. On the wrong day, even a parking ticket can send us into a state of financial panic. The ticket triggers all the other money worries we've suppressed, and by the time we get home we're thoroughly out of sorts and ready to impose a ridiculous thrift regimen on our family. We have become the victims of money. It seems that money will always be a source of worry and anxiety, an unbeatable foe rather than the helpful ally it should be.

We all feel this way at times, but some people feel it all the time. Unlike the Dodger, who retains enough control to function adequately, if not well, the Victim is chronically unable to take control of his financial life, and his inability frequently gets him into trouble.

Why should a person be so financially out of control that one crisis generates another? In attempting to understand the Victim, we can identify essentially two types: those born to the role, and those who volunteer for it.

In the first group we often find children of the once rich, who grew up neither worrying about nor learning how to handle money. Nor did they ever expect they would have to learn. When their family lost its money these people were cast adrift, unable to learn quickly abilities that others acquired over many years.

Also in this group are many women who as girls were taught to let men take care of money and weren't taught to handle it themselves. Women weren't supposed to worry about all those numbers and problems—that was men's work. By the time a woman brought up this way decides or needs to know, she lacks the confidence, experience, and training to take charge.

Those who volunteer for the role of Victim are usually people who don't want to grow up. They hold onto the child's position of dependency well into adulthood, and money is an effective tool with which to do that. Taking care of money is a task for grown-ups, not children. Such people are victimized repeatedly by their own passive hope that they can remain dependent forever, that some guardian angel will take care of them. Their hopeful, if foolish agreement with money is that if they don't take care of money, money will take care of them.

Some of these people do indeed find their guardian angel—a friend, a spouse, a boss. Unfortunately, some of them find exploitative predators more than willing to demonstrate that the world will not take care of them forever.

And so the pattern goes, one disaster after another. With luck, sooner or later the voluntary Victim goes through the difficult experience of learning how to look after himself. But that can take a long time, with many painful lessons along the way.

The crux of the problem, again, is not intellectual or economic, but emotional. Giving up the dependent position is difficult for all of us but extremely difficult for the Victim, so much so that he chooses the pain of victimization over the pain he imagines would accompany taking charge. To the Victim, being able to deal with money means independence, a state he fears. So he sets up his agreement to perpetuate a dependent state. He says, "I won't take control of you. In exchange, you will leave me helpless and in need of someone to save me."

Viewed in these terms, the Victim becomes less puzzling. We would all occasionally like to return to the time when we were taken care of. We would all occasionally like to rid ourselves of financial responsibilities. But most of us learn that assuming those responsibilities is nowhere as difficult as we imagined it would be. Like so many steps in life, the *idea* of taking charge turns out to be more frightening than doing it.

With encouragement and reassurance, the Victim can begin to master his own financial fate, replacing the dependent stance with a more independent one. As he begins to realize that he can do that, he will enjoy his mastery. It's a common psychological mistake to say that victims like being victims. They choose that position because, for them, it's the less miserable and more familiar alternative. As the financial Victim discovers he is capable of greater control and independence, he will give up his passive stance enthusiastically. He chose it originally only because of emotional necessity.

From Victim to Victor: Developing a Sound Financial Lifestyle

Harry McBride, thirty-four, is a designer for a telecommunications business in southeast Florida. His salary of $53,000 is the lowest of his colleagues. Although many consider Harry the most creative and talented mind in the firm, he allows himself to be taken advantage of in salary negotiations, preferring to be a "nice guy" to being paid what he's worth. He feels victimized and berates himself for not being more aggressive. He loves his job, except the part that deals with competing, or money, or negotiating. Harry's rich mother's constant pep talks about how to do better only make him feel worse. Harry has about $150,000 of the $225,000 his grandmother left him five years ago; he keeps it in a money market fund and makes withdrawals whenever he feels the need. Seventy-five thousand dollars has been frittered away on bad investments and his annual economic shortfall.

Harry's attempts to improve his overall financial situation have failed. He once bought a stock on a tip from his brother, an investment broker. When it immediately went down in price a little Harry sold it in a panic, only to see the stock rise as his brother held onto it. He joined a group of friends who were buying a house to hold as an income-generating rental property. Just as they were about to close on the deal, the house burned to the ground. Shaken, Harry withdrew his money and now kicks himself as the second property they bought has done very well. He likes to go to the track because he occasionally wins there, but over the course of a year he drops about $500. Whenever he buys anything, from clothes to a car to technical equipment, he automatically assumes he'll get gypped, so he never shops around. He finds bargain hunting distasteful.

Generous to a fault, Harry gives away a lot of his money. At the Monday morning meeting of the graphics department, it's always Harry who brings the refreshments. Extremely popular around the office, he pays attention to everyone and often takes the secretaries out for lunch. His colleagues are a heavy-drinking bunch after work, and Harry always picks up more than his share of the tab. Although he enjoys giving, he resents the fact that the others never insist on being as generous as he is.

His brother has frequently offered to help him, but when it comes time to take decisive action, Harry balks. He jokes about his bad luck and openly calls himself "a loser." While others admire him for his talent, he downgrades himself for his lack of financial success. His defeatist attitude has reached Woody Allen proportions. "I'm a self-defeating personality," he says, and when others point out his artistic success he adds, "and I can't even do self-defeat right."

He sometimes has trouble paying his bills, and he resents the fact that others less talented make more. But he is unable to take control, either by reducing his spending or by aggressively going after a raise, or by investing his money to provide a greater return.

How can a victim like Harry manage his money? Some psychotherapy might help him, but barring that, what should he do? His best bet is to begin to take control in small matters. When the tab arrives he doesn't have to pull out his calculator, but he could make an effort to figure his own share and then contribute that much. He could ask to be reimbursed for the Monday morning doughnuts rather than wait for someone to offer. And he should give up the track. It's a haven for passive victims.

Instead of literally investing in a loser image, Harry could *let* himself try winning, or at least breaking even. Rather than enter into every purchase with the assumption that he'll get ripped off, he could try shopping around, making it a rule to compare at least two prices before making a large purchase. He doesn't have to become a cutthroat shopper for his savings over the course of a year to become considerable. More important is the psychological boost it would give Harry to discover he doesn't have to be such a chump.

The same principle applies to negotiating for a better salary. But rather than go one-on-one with his boss, a battle he's repeatedly lost, Harry could approach other firms and see what they might be willing to pay him. There's no rule against seeing what's out there, although many victims behave as if there were. If Harry gets a better offer he'd be in a good position to negotiate with his boss. Although he shouldn't deliver an ultimatum unless he's prepared to leave, he could at least let it be known that he has a better offer elsewhere.

As Harry strives to become more independent and assertive, he might be helped by the encouragement and advice of a good financial planner. Although generally reserved for people wealthier than Harry, he may make use of the consultation. Harry's brother can recommend a good one, since he's in the financial field himself. More than most people, a Victim needs help in avoiding schemes and people who may harm him financially.

Finding a Financial Planner

A financial planner is someone you go to when your financial life—bills, budgeting, insurance, taxes, investments, etc.—seems to be getting out of control. This person is a generalist who examines everything in your life that has to do with money and then formulates a plan to help you meet your financial goals.

The best way to find a good financial planner is the same

way you probably found your doctor, lawyer, or plumber: a referral from a friend whose judgment you respect. But before you sign up, there are a few things you should know about this field.

If you ask a financial planner exactly what he does, he'll try to give you the impression that he's some kind of skilled money doctor who will cure all your ills—true only of a few. First, the term itself means very little. Anyone can call himself a financial planner and go into business overnight. There is no licensing procedure whatsoever. With the 1980s bull market and the explosion of the financial services industry, there are hundreds of thousands of financial planners ready to advise you today who were not financial planners yesterday.

There is, moreover, no regulation of the industry, and a virtual epidemic of lawsuits by customers of financial planners is jamming the courts. The vast majority of planners are not objective in the advice they give, and their tie-in to the investments they recommend isn't always that obvious. Truly objective and competent financial planners are often very expensive.

If you go to a stockbroker (or a car salesman, for that matter) you know from the start that he wants to sell you something. That's how he makes his living; you know it and he knows it. There's no fee for his time. Financial planners, on the other hand, appear to be objective because they generally do charge a fee for their time (usually $50 to $100 an hour). But for most of them, that's just the beginning. Unlike your doctor's prescription, your financial planner's prescription often is his bread and butter; it produces as much as 90 percent of his income. Their recommendations for what you need frequently turn out to be high-commission mutual fund and insurance products, to be purchased through the planner, of course.

The financial planning industry is troubled by its image

and legal disputes, and is attempting to establish some semblance of organization, certification, and self-regulation. A small percentage of planners are now "certified" planners: they have taken a correspondence course and passed a financial planning exam.

Harry should look for a "fee-only" planner—one who doesn't sell any investments. Not surprisingly, fee-only advisers don't necessarily recommend an investment as the solution to every problem. Setting up a family corporation or trust account, for example, might be recommended as a way of sheltering taxes instead of some high-commission investment. Harry can be helped both in curbing his expenditures and in making investments—safe ones, rather like those of Hank the Pessimist. His financial planner might suggest real estate as an investment, or tax-free municipal bonds.

Sometimes financial planners are promised a percentage of a sponsor's profits for pointing their clients toward a certain investment deal. Harry should ask if his planner will be getting any compensation on the recommendations he makes.

A small percentage of planners have joined the National Association of Personal Financial Advisers (125 S. Wilke Road, Arlington Heights, IL 60005), which requires a strict fee-only practice.

A Computerized Plan

Harry may be tempted to try a computerized financial plan. These plans, offered by banks, brokers, and insurance companies, range in price from $50 to $500 and are targeted primarily at people in the $50,000 to $150,000 income level. You fill out a long questionnaire, send it in, wait about a month, and get back a slick report (fifteen to seventy-five pages, depending on the price of the plan) telling you everything you ever wanted to know about how to survive life's financial pitfalls. Your net worth is neatly calculated; all kinds of insurance needs are figured for you; taxes are estimated; retirement plans are analyzed; investment strategies are laid out; estate plans are set, and so on.

The onetime exercise of having all your financial data gathered and organized, so that you know where you stand, is helpful and revealing for many people (most plans will update annually for a reduced fee). The problem with these plans is the same as that of many of the more expensive, more personalized ones provided by financial planners: lack of objectivity. The computerized plans are often sales tools for the companies and agents sponsoring them. So you wind up paying $300 to help your insurance agent prove to you that you need to buy more insurance or to help your broker prove that what you really need is more municipal bonds.

Whomever Harry hires, there's only one sure way to get the most out of him. When you consult with any financial adviser, make sure that you let him know about everything—not only your resources and goals but your money style and your agreement with money as well. It may take a search to find a person open to this kind of approach, but if you can find him the dividends should be enormous.

If you're a Gambler let him know that so he can put some limits on you. If he takes advantage of your tendency, encouraging you to gamble more, get rid of him fast. If you're a Pessimist or a Worrier—someone inclined to be overly cautious—let your adviser know that, so he can encourage you toward reasonable risk. If you're an Overspender tell him so that he can set up your funds so they're harder for you to get at. If you're a Dodger or a Victim like Harry who would like to change, tell your adviser that you want to become educated about your money. Make sure that he's willing to take the time to explain his actions so that you can, in time, move out of this category.

As Harry gains confidence, he should be aware of the people who are closest to him. Families of a Victim often want, consciously or unconsciously, to keep him in his place. If he gains enough confidence to make more investment decisions on his own, Harry should be alert to those predators who prey on Victims: overly aggressive brokers, get-rich-quick scheme artists, and the racetrack. If he does learn to invest wisely the money he saves by not giving it away or by selling himself cheap, Harry can begin to transform himself from a financial loser into a winner. He can keep his Woody Allen shtick if he likes, but he should remember that Woody Allen is not poor.

The Depressive

We're all familiar with depression. At one time or another probably everyone has been depressed. Although the syndrome is personal in its details, its general features include a pervasive lack of interest, fatigue, feelings of hopelessness and pessimism, self-degradation, inattention to others. Physical symptoms include loss of energy, appetite, sleep, and sexual desire. In its extreme form, depression requires psychiatric intervention. In its milder form, people live through it.

For the occasionally depressed person, money—shopping and spending—can be an antidepressant. For the Depressive, it doesn't help. Like most other things, money ceases to be of interest to the Depressive. It is just another bother, another meaningless encumbrance, another nagging voice from the outside world.

The Depressive's attitude about money makes him vulnerable. A person whose motto is, "Why bother?" may miss important opportunities, let critical obligations pass, or be taken advantage of. When we hear about gross financial errors in business for families, we usually hear only the financial facts: "How could he have been so dumb?" "Can you believe she let that get past her?" We usually don't hear about the blunderer's emotional state. He may have been functioning poorly because of severe depression. Normally, it's not intelligence that falters but the emotional energy needed to activate that intelligence. A depressed person is passive, goes through the motions, but isn't really there. Whatever his agreement may have been it becomes, "I don't care." It is essential for another person to protect the Depressive from his apathetic nonagreement. His unconscious wish, reflected in his nonagreement, is to punish himself, usually out of a pervasive sense of guilt. Unfortunately, money provides a ready means of self-punishment.

The only way to avoid disaster is to recognize that depression is present—not easy because both the sufferer and those around him often pretend it isn't there. Depression threatens everyone's equilibrium, which is why we usually avoid a person who is sad.

It's important to acknowledge depression and to get appropriate help for it. Because the Depressive isn't himself, money matters are best taken over by a trusted and qualified person. Depression almost always passes, with or without help, although help can make it pass sooner. The most important thing is to make sure that disaster doesn't occur in the meantime.

The Manic

Of the many money styles we've described, this is the only one that in its severe form constitutes a major mental illness. The manic state is characterized by extreme agitation and physical restlessness, rapid speech that often sounds as if it were being pumped out by a fevered brain, an inability to sleep, a tendency to skip from one topic to another not incoherently but rapidly, as if there weren't enough time to fit everything in, exaggerated feelings of personal importance, a propensity for making big plans, especially travel— and spending lots and lots of money. A person experiencing a manic episode can go through an entire fortune in an afternoon.

Sufferers of manic-depressive illness (technically called Bipolar Affective Disorder) often have dynamic, creative personalities; they may do extremely well, particularly in people-oriented fields like sales. When they become manic they often do themselves and their businesses considerable damage.

Dorothy Johnson was thirty-seven, married to a lawyer, and the mother of two teenage sons. She had risen through the ranks to become regional director of a nationwide real-estate company. Her phenomenal sales record made people forget her periodic instability when she drank or became bizarrely gregarious. Her husband found her moods trying, but he knew he wasn't the easiest person to live with himself, and he chalked it up to the way life turns out.

Suffering from undiagnosed manic-depressive illness, Dorothy dealt with the highs and lows by self-medicating herself with vodka, and it worked pretty well for many years. A Bloody Mary for breakfast gave fair warning to her children to steer clear of Mom that day. Vivacious and charming, she had managed to persuade more than a few policemen to overlook the fact that she was driving under the influence. She avoided her family physician, who had told her to join AA. Most of her friends were heavy drinkers, too, and she had learned remarkably well to work while intoxicated.

Everything was generally fine until a major manic episode hit. It began with a cleanup campaign. Husband and sons were awakened at 1 a.m., told to "hit the deck," and given their orders. When they tried to dissuade Dorothy she threatened physical violence. At work she tore through the week trying to outdo her own sales record. Her secretary could tell something was very wrong when she got a call from a restaurant in Paris confirming a luncheon reservation booked a week hence for the entire office.

Then a full-page ad appeared in the Sunday paper, in color, with photos of six of the most expensive homes in the city, none of which was for sale. The headline read: "BY 5 P.M., THESE HOUSES WILL BE SOLD!" Dorothy had paid for the ad herself, in cash.

Over the course of the next week Dorothy liquidated all of her assets, including selling the family home, which was in her name, in order to buy a small magazine so that she could publish her husband's poetry.

By the time Dorothy was hospitalized, she apparently had lost her job, her house, and her money—all in less than a week. Luckily, most of the damage was undone. The people who bought her house agreed to cancel the contract; the people whose houses were advertised were persuaded not to sue; the magazine voided the sale. And Dorothy's family began to learn about manic-depressive illness.

Money fits so "well" into this syndrome because it can provide such immediate access to grandeur. The essence of mania is flight: flight of ideas, flight of emotion, flight from sadness to greatness. I can't stand the pain, the manic says, so I will fly, often on the wings of money, to a grander plane; I will outrun and outgrow my pain. And for a few minutes, the strategy works. The hard part is cleaning up the mess afterward.

Once the diagnosis is made, the condition can be treated chemically with a drug called lithium and socially with limits and support. The key is to make the diagnosis before catastrophe occurs.

Eighteen

The Overspender

This category includes just about everybody. At one time or another, all of us have spent more than we can afford, or more than we have. Almost everybody incurs debt; indeed, it's the national pastime. Where would we be without our plastic?

In its most common, moderate version, overspending makes sense; to support a family it's almost a necessity. Usually the Overspender thinks of money as a useful tool, if one that's always in too-short supply. Overspending becomes a motive to work harder, to continue to grow. It fits in with the part of the American character that believes in working toward a solid future, and it usually works to a person's advantage so long as it doesn't become extreme. Unlike the Gambler, who often risks for the sake of risk rather than profit, the Overspender takes calculated risks, operating on such conventional wisdom as, "You've got to spend money to make money," or, "Good things last longer."

In its mildest form, the Overspender's agreement with money is fairly innocuous: "If I spend you, you will make me feel better." If the Overspender is able to cope with the tension mild debt creates, he or she usually reaps benefits down the line. The style becomes disabling only when it veers off in one of two directions: either the real debt becomes too great, or the ability to cope becomes too small.

If, for example, you're by nature a cautious person averse to risk and you give in to the pressure of peers, a spouse, or a general bullish *Zeitgeist,* you may soon find yourself incurring what seems to you terrifyingly large debt, from mortgage to car to credit cards to short-term loans. Suddenly you feel as if you have no control over your financial life. This can quickly translate into sleepless nights, general irritability, and a sense of panic that begins to prevail not just over money but all aspects of your life—you have become a Worrier.

Some Overspenders do what they do in order to maintain a position of discomfort, creating in their financial life the same mild deprivation they experience emotionally. Few people get as much love or approval as they want. By overspending we create that same feeling of not having quite enough, which we believe we can cure by buying things.

Overspending may become a means of dealing with depression. That isn't to say that buying is invariably a way of handling an underlying sadness. But there is a kind of behavior psychiatrists call action defense, an action that defends against emotions we don't wish to feel. Workaholism and overeating are action defenses. When overspending functions in this way, the result usually is a brief lifting of mood, followed by deeper depression.

What begins with a bad mood in the morning turns into an afternoon shopping spree. The Overspender is dimly aware of what he or she is doing, but manages to repress reason. If you can't have a decent relationship at least you can have some decent clothes. Spending is both a distraction from depression and a mild turn-on, a sort of subtle autoeroticism. The process begins with a magical hope: that supplies are without limit. Aided by the magic wand of the credit card, we buy—and it's great fun. Who needs approval from others when you can cart home all this stuff for free? Or so it seems.

Usually the Overspender doesn't let the process get out of hand. As soon as the bills come in, he gets that familiar feeling of self-recrimination, and a limit is set—only to be broken later on. Sometimes, however, the limit isn't set; particularly among women, spending may become an active replacement for love. (When men feel unloved they're more likely to throw themselves into work and make more money, or to have an affair.) Indeed, some people are as addicted to spending as others are to drugs, with equally self-destructive results. Chronic, unmanageable debt is truly disabling. Why would anyone willingly put himself into it?

Again, the answer lies in a misalignment of emotions and money. The hope is that money can cure depression. When a little fails, try more. Rather than looking for an emotional cure to an emotional problem, the Overspender looks for a fiscal cure, which is like trying to change a tire with a shoehorn.

The Overspender often acts on a contradictory premise: "I have enough money/I don't have enough money." The side that feels it has enough money buys and buys and buys; the side that feels it doesn't have enough money frets and frets and frets. This is the fellow who takes out his calculator to divide up a check one week and buys himself a car the next. How he acts depends on which side is in control.

The two sides often don't speak to each other. One day the "I have enough" side swings into action: a shopping spree, a vacation, a new car. The next day the "I don't have enough" side cries out in pain—and sometimes this results in action, like second mortgages or liquidating assets.

The obvious solution is to have a meeting, or at least a conference call, between the two sides. The Enough side might point out to the Not Enough side that matters aren't as bleak as they seem and promise to try to consult prior to purchase in the future. The Not Enough side ought to agree to send cautionary messages before the fact, when they can do some good.

Tightening the Money Belt: Developing a Sound Financial Lifestyle

Laurie and Joel Bacon live in a suburb of Boston with their two-year-old daughter, Rebecca. Laurie, who's thirty-three, completed her residency in psychiatry three years ago and is now in private practice. She's also in training to become an analyst, which means undergoing a personal training analysis (four sessions a week at $90 a session) that will last at least a few years. Her income is $70,000 a year after office overhead.

Joel, who is thirty-seven, is also an M.D.; he practices internal medicine in the same office building where Laurie works. They own the building with two other doctors, having borrowed from Laurie's parents to make the down payment. Joel, who has been in practice six years, makes $105,000 a year after office overhead.

Laurie and Joel love to have fun. Although they both work hard, they also love to play. While they were dating when Joel was a resident and Laurie a medical student they were known as "party central," and people still count on their dance parties as guaranteed uppers.

Joel, who grew up rich, saw his family lose almost all their money through neglect. He still feels rich in his bones, although he has no money behind him, having spent the last of his inheritance as the down payment on the house he bought for $125,000 in 1982.

Laurie, who grew up in a middle-income family, likes her mother's motto, "You can't take it with you." She has a tendency toward depression, but finds the life they lead a good antidote to sadness.

171

Joel and Laurie have known for some time that something was off financially. They were pleased that they owned two pieces of real estate, but not only weren't they saving anything, they even had to borrow to make ends meet. They had borrowed money to cover one-time-only expenses like furniture for the house and office, baby paraphernalia, and the like, and had used up $100,000 of the home-equity credit-line loan they had taken on their house. And their plastic was pushed to the credit limit. They took turns worrying about their problem until one day Laurie made an appointment with a financial planner. He asked them to bring their checkbook and their past three years' tax returns.

In the course of much embarrassed shifting about in their chairs, Laurie and Joel discovered what they hadn't known before—how much they spent. Now, when they added it up, this is how it looked on a monthly basis (using round numbers):

Home mortgage on $250,000	$ 2,500
Laurie's psychoanalysis	1,500
Insurance	2,000
Rent (office)	1,500
Car loans and maintenance	350
Babysitter	1,000
Telephone, yard, utilities, heat	500
Food (eating in)	500
Travel and entertainment	1,000
Taxes	2,500
Clothes	600
Gifts (toys, friends)	250
Donations	250
Books, journals, papers	250
Total	$ 14,700 a month
	$176,400 a year

With a combined income of $175,000, Laurie and Joel were in the red.

They felt ashamed, guilty and embarrassed. Laurie told Joel he should get into psychoanalysis, and Joel told Laurie if she'd get out maybe they'd have some money. The financial planner intervened and told them they weren't alone. Lots of people who make plenty of money still manage to overspend it.

Joel and Laurie, and others like them, are hardly a lost cause, at least not yet. The house Joel wisely bought before they got married has risen in value to $400,000, so they still have $150,000 in equity there. Their share of the office building is worth another $200,000, and they get a good tax deduction from it. By any reckoning, they're very well off for a young couple.

If they can come to terms with the emotional basis of their overspending and if they're ready to make some changes, there can be a good prognosis.

The first step that Laurie and Joel took was to find out where the money was going. This was a real shock, as it is for many people. So long as they didn't know the numbers, they could make believe the money was simply "disappearing." Once they saw the numbers, they had to acknowledge they were spending it. The Overspender's refrain, "Where does it all go?" has an answer if he looks for it. Many Overspenders, like Laurie and Joel, keep almost no records, which makes expenditures hard to track down, but canceled checks, credit card statements, and bank and tax records can piece most of it together.

The next step for Joel and Laurie is to give themselves some credit, as it were. They've worked hard and done well. Much of their overspending has been either in the service of further training (her analysis), or giving pleasure to others (their entertainment bill), or in getting quality care for their daughter. Hardly a life of high sin. And, as Laurie's mother says, "You can't take it with you."

On the other hand, Laurie and Joel agree it's time to change, and having figured out where it goes, the issue is where to cut. Budgeting is like dieting—the best way isn't to go on a crash diet but to change your eating habits. Joel and Laurie have to alter their spending habits to effect lasting change. As with many people their age, their incomes should continue to grow, so that if they redirect their spending now they will be in excellent shape over the long run.

The first thing Laurie and Joel ought to do is to realign their monthly expenditures into sub-categories based on need. This would give them a better idea of where spending reductions can be made immediately, where future reductions could be made, and which items are basically nonnegotiable. Here's how their chart might look:

Fixed monthly payments that can't be reduced without principal repayments to lower the debt:

	Current Monthly	*New Goal*
Mortgage	$2,500	$2,500
Malpractice insurance	2,000	2,000
Office overhead	1,500	1,500
Car loan	300	300
Car maintenance	50	50
Medical insurance	50	50

Temporary monthly payment that will be eliminated in two years, allowing for a significant reduction in expenses:

Laurie's analysis	1,500	1,500

174

Necessary items that could be reduced with careful planning, some sacrifice, and the use of cash rather than credit:

Groceries	500	400	more careful spending
Utilities, phone	350	300	slight reduction possible
House maintenance	150	50	do more themselves
Babysitting	1,000	500	some use of day care center
Clothing	600	300	do with less for now
Books, journals	250	50	use the medical library

Discretionary items that could be greatly reduced temporarily until their income/outflow is well under control:

Travel	600	300	learn to enjoy home more
Entertainment	400	200	find less costly means
Gifts	250	100	spend too much here anyway
Donations	250	50	make it up later

Current Monthly Expenses (Before Taxes) $12,250
Projected Monthly Expenses (Before Taxes) $10,150

Projected Monthly Savings Through Budgeting $2,100–$25,200 a year

A Savings Plan for Joel and Laurie

Set up enforced savings. With a reduction in their monthly spending of $2,100, Joel and Laurie can afford to make a significant contribution to a retirement plan. This would, in turn, reduce their final and largest expense item: taxes.

By contributing $1,500 of their $2,100 monthly savings directly into a Keogh plan, they would reduce their monthly tax bill by approximately $400, or $4,800 a year. This extra savings would increase their total monthly savings from $2,100 to $2,500.

Here's how the $2,500 a month should be allocated:

Keogh plan	$1,500
Custodian account for Rebecca	500
Illiquid savings account	500

The key to this plan is to make the monthly savings automatic and illiquid. Laurie and Joel can accomplish this
reduction of disposable income by opening these three
accounts and by directing their bank to disperse three payments a month, right off the top of their income before any
bills are paid or discretionary income is spent. They should
not allow a checkbook to the savings account to be issued,
and they should make sure there are severe penalties for
withdrawing from these accounts.

Believe it or not, if they're like most people Laurie and
Joel will quickly adjust. The difference between living on
$175,000 and $145,000 for a young couple with a pre-
schoolchild is more a matter of perspective than of eco-
nomics. Surely when they were making $50,000, $145,000
seemed like a lot of income.

Simply earning interest is good enough for the first year
in each of these three accounts. Once the money has built
up, they can look into various investment strategies that
might enable them to get a higher rate of return.

Cancel lines of credit. Credit cards are dangerous for Overspenders. Laurie and Joel should pay off and close out any
major credit card or store charge account that isn't absolutely necessary and start paying most of their bills with cash
or check. A single charge card, preferably one that doesn't
extend monthly credit, suffices for most people.

By reducing their sources of credit, Joel and Laurie cannot only free themselves from the vicious cycle of eternally
compounding debt (at the very highest interest rates), but
they also can go a long way in relieving themselves of the
guilt and anxiety of living above their means.

Don't increase spending in proportion to increased income. Two
years from now Joel and Laurie will have a significant
increase in cash flow. When Laurie completes her analytic
training, the Bacons will be freed of an $18,000 a year
financial burden. Assuming the training will allow her to

charge more for her own services (and that she will be able to find patients to fill the hours that ending her analysis will free up), Laurie's income could increase as much as her expenses decrease. If Joel's practice also continues to grow, his income will be greater two years from now as well.

Like many couples, Laurie and Joel have always spent more money as they've made more, dollar for dollar. This habit must change. The most constructive way to do this is for them to commit right now to making major debt-reducing payments against their mortgages and their car loans as soon as their cash flow starts increasing.

Budgets aren't meant to take all the fun out of life. The Bacons can certainly increase their spending—gradually and under control—as the years pass. But their lives will improve significantly in terms of increasing security and decreasing anxiety if they apply a little self-discipline now.

How (and Why) to Make a Budget

Other than winning the lottery or inheriting or marrying money, there really are only three honest ways to improve your financial lot: by earning more, by investing more wisely, and by spending less. If you don't have a lot of capital to invest, and if you're not about to change jobs or otherwise increase your inflow of money, you unfortunately must concentrate on controlling your outflow and living within your means if you want to brighten your financial picture. The rational plan you must draw up is known as (ugh) a budget.

For most people, keeping track of spending isn't that necessary because they just sense how much they can spend without going overboard. This is true for people at all income levels. But the Overspender, or the person with another dominant style but with overspending tendencies, often feels impelled to get rid of every dollar he makes, and then some. The damage can be great.

The beginning stages of rationally budgeting your money

177

can be painful. The Overspender must face the fact that he cannot afford all the things that make him feel temporarily secure or important (or worthy or powerful or happy). There may be a lot of facing up to do, as well as a lot of priority shifting. The Overspender must come to realize that he doesn't need to spend so much, and maybe he doesn't even want to spend so much. Perhaps that new car isn't all that great anyway. Maybe it won't make him feel any better. In fact, what would really make him feel better is not being so deeply in debt. Similarly, those credit card purchases probably aren't worth the stress they always cause in his marriage. A good relationship and peace of mind will ultimately prove more important than unnecessary purchases.

Learning to live within your means is a great step in self-acceptance. Many very rich people aren't flashy at all with their money. Take the cars they drive—old Fords or Volvos. Their self-esteem doesn't derive from their possessions: everyone knows they can drive any car they want to.

The greatest obstacles to setting up and maintaining a budget are psychological. Budgets are messy—all those numbers! Budgets are not sexy. Budgets hear bad news— who wants to see it laid out in black and white that you can't afford your thousand-dollar-a-month VISA bill? Budgets set limits—who wants to be told what to do, especially with his money?

Making a budget, like making any resolution, represents an attempt by the ego—the adult inside you—to mediate between the forces of the id (the infant) and the superego (the punishing parent). Unfortunately, in sticking to most resolutions, the poor old ego gets overwhelmed from both sides. The id bursts through and we act, breaking the resolution. Then the superego goes to town, berating us for our sins.

Throughout this book we have attempted to team up with

your financial ego. A budget is simply an external aid for the ego in its struggle to mediate. It can best be adhered to if the goals are modest and support is abundant.

The upside of adhering to a budget—and you have to be convinced of this before a budget can become anything but a guilt-provoking broken resolution—is that budgets can make you better off. Remember, you make the budget. You are setting the limits. You are taking control. It isn't a matter of deprivation—you can splurge with the money you save if you'd like to. Wouldn't you rather have a Caribbean vacation than the two dozen incidental purchases you made on MasterCard that you didn't need?

The emotional illusion is that the budget will tie you up. The reality is that it can help untie you from wasteful habits you don't notice.

As the "therapy" goes on and your financial situation improves, you may begin to discover underlying reasons for your overspending, from an inherited family style, to a competitive urge to keep up with the Joneses, to underlying intermittent depression, to boredom. You can take rational steps to address these problems as well. And you will be better equipped to do that as you spend less time either overspending or worrying about overspending. By beginning with a rational plan, something as simple as a budget, you can alter your financial life as well as your emotional life.

Nineteen

Do You Really Want
to Be Rich?

Are the Rich Really Different from
You and Me?

That money has no absolute psychological value becomes clear when we try to define "rich." How much is rich? To a child, a $5 bill can represent a vast fortune. To an executive, a six-figure salary can mean just getting by. To a family that was once extremely wealthy, even having to think about money may feel like humiliating poverty. Yet even though we lack an exact number that differentiates rich from poor, no one would deny there is a difference.

Except that they have more money than the rest of us, is there anything all rich people have in common? Probably not—except our fascination with them. We love to read about them, talk about them, observe them in their native habitat through whatever peepholes the media can provide. Few details about a person can capture our attention more quickly than his or her wealth.

It disappoints us to imagine that rich people are subject to the same laws of nature the rest of us endure, so we focus on what they don't have to put up with. They don't have to do laundry. They don't have to stand in line at the Department of Motor Vehicles for an hour only to be told they were in the wrong line. They can get tickets to anything; maybe they don't even need tickets. They don't have to search for a parking space; they don't even have to drive if they don't want to. They don't pay their own bills. Balance a checkbook? The only thing they balance is a drink in one hand and a canapé in the other.

It's hard for us to imagine that rich people worry. If they do it's mostly about global problems like hunger or nuclear war, or about inconsequentials, like who has the biggest diamond. They don't worry in the ordinary, boring way the rest of us do about college tuitions or whether we have enough insurance.

We have other ideas about rich people, too. Most of the rich are cheap, which is how they got rich and how they stay that way. They're also paranoid: they don't trust anybody because they think everybody is out to get their money. That's why they don't have any friends except other rich people. They get together at incredibly lavish dinner parties and talk about rich topics like pheasants and presidents and why Washington doesn't have a baseball team, things they don't really care about. They don't really care about anything because they're so rich they haven't suffered enough for anything to matter much.

They look different, too. Their markings are hard to describe. It's more of a glow, a self-assurance that's embedded in their blood cells. They never worry about being socially inappropriate because whatever they do defines social appropriateness. The ones who inherited their money are all alcoholic wastrels. And the ones who earned it themselves are narrow and ruthless. All of which is to say that we love them and we hate them. It's as difficult to forgive them for being rich as it is to admit they might be human after all.

181

Do You Sincerely Want to Be Rich?

Money, like most things, has its cycles of popularity. A mere twenty years after being thoroughly out of favor, the pursuit of money is very much back in favor. Everyone is looking for the quick route to success, the big score. Almost every young person believes, however briefly, in the possibility of being rich.

There's a real basis for that belief. The inflation-filled 1970s will always be remembered in financial history as the days of instant real-estate tycoons, a thirty-year-old millionaire on every city block. The 1980s bull market created even greater opportunities for people on Wall Street. Those years of unprecedented riches have whipped Americans into a frenzy of belief that money can be created overnight out of nothing.

In this book we have met people like the Hustler and Icarus, who feel there's a race going on in life and that the prize for winning is money—money that will bring power, self-esteem, specialness. What qualities separate the winners from the losers in that race? And is the race worth running in the first place?

Not everyone really wants to be rich: the determining factor, as we have seen, lies in a person's agreement with money. Most people aren't willing to compromise what they consider the more important parts of their lives—relationships, family, health, personal integrity, liking what they do for a living—to improve their financial status. Not all people who have made themselves rich have bad marriages or are less than honest, of course, but the money-driven do know where their priorities lie. "Really wanting" to be rich might be defined as not only placing a high priority on money but also being willing, if necessary, to compromise those other, important aspects of life.

Most people who have made a great deal of money have made significant sacrifices somewhere along the way. They may, for instance, have worked for years at jobs they didn't like in order to get to the right point for financial take-off. They may have spent an inordinate amount of time worrying about money and obsessing over financial matters in order to be more aware of investment opportunities than the rest of us are.

There are several reasons that some people get rich and others don't. The first is that it takes money to make money.

Capital and Leverage

Starting out poor and ending up rich is a great American dream. As it turns out, though, most rich people were at least moderately well off to begin with. Getting rich usually requires a lot of planning ahead and a certain amount of capital to invest, both of which are just about impossible for the poor. Most rich people started off with at least a high-income job, and even there they realized that getting truly rich as employees or sole practitioners was nearly impossible.

Most people can make a good living if they work hard and have a good reputation, but few of them earn a cent when they're not in their office. More important, none of them owns any equity in his business that can be left to family or sold to someone else on retirement. All a practitioner usually owns is the value of his daily services.

How does a professional go from comfortable to rich, then? The rare stockbroker splits off and starts his own specialty investment business. The real-estate lawyer becomes a developer himself after years of serving other developers. The doctor starts an HMO. All of them build equity in their businesses that they can eventually cash in on. But even here a certain amount of capital was required: each had enough savings to forgo current income during the early years of his new enterprise, and each was willing to put in another requirement of getting rich—hard work.

Hard Work

Self-made rich people have almost always worked harder than people who aren't rich. Almost everyone has the fantasy, but very few are willing to pay this particular price.

Hard work, combined with a good business sense and a certain amount of capital, is the surest path to wealth. Consider the unlikely alternatives of dreamers: great talent that somehow happens to get utilized, or an investment flier that just happens to work out spectacularly. Neither is very likely.

Good Sense

There certainly is a correlation between intelligence and money: most high-income people are well-educated and intelligent. But everyone knows both exceptions to the rule: your rich friend, who isn't half as smart as you are; and your brilliant friend, whose investment decisions you watch like a hawk so you can do just the opposite.

Common sense, street savvy, and a good feel for human nature are often more useful than education and intellect when it comes to succeeding with money. Many otherwise intelligent people go blindly into investments they know nothing about and often let pride and emotional considerations get in the way of rational decision-making. To a large extent, such decision-making is what this book is all about.

Overcoming Fear and Greed

Fear and greed are exactly what the stock market is all about. Fear is what motivates sellers, and greed is what motivates buyers. But an excess of either prevents many people from getting anywhere financially.

The successful Gambler knows that most people who go after high-risk investments with emotion instead of reason end up losing their money. But the possibility of a quick gain has too much appeal for many people to turn down. Greed is what makes these otherwise intelligent people go into dumb, sometimes crooked investment deals. The list of well-known people who have been suckered into investment scams is startling. How could people with a lot of business experience and plenty of financial advice available to them go into such obviously stupid deals? The answer is simple: greed won out over rationality once again.

Fear is just as great a detriment as greed to making money. The Worrier, the Pessimist, the Dodger, and the Victim generally find ordinary risk too terrifying to handle. Yet they are often the first to complain about missed opportunities. Few of the fearful ever become rich.

Both the fearful and the greedy suffer from the oldest hazard in any marketplace: the influence of mass psychology. As the stock market drops lower and lower, the fear level of most investors increases. At the very moment the cool, streetwise pro licks his chops for opportunities in a deeply depressed market, the timid investor throws in the towel, no matter what the cost is, in order to salvage what he can (as witnessed on October 19, 1987). The same is true at the top, after a long and sustained bull market. Just as the wise old pro knows it's time to take his profits, many investors, having watched the market go up without them, convince themselves it's finally safe again and plunge back in just as the market peaks.

Connections

Businessmen don't join country clubs just for the golf and tennis. Being around other people who have money—and good ideas and good connections of their own—creates opportunities for the person intent on getting ahead financially.

School connections can be tremendously helpful. Some

185

say the greatest benefit of going to Harvard Business School is the lifelong access to classmates and other alumni around the country who themselves become business leaders.

Where you live, whom you marry, where your kids go to school, the friends you make, how you spend your leisure time, even where you take your vacations can affect your economic status and financial opportunities.

Luck

Luck certainly plays a role in financial success and failure. In some areas, notably the stock market, it plays a major role. Legions of young real-estate mavens in the seventies made a lot of money simply by being there. Most of them knew next to nothing about real estate, but the combination of leverage and high inflation worked magic. The same was true in the stock market in the 1980s. The average stock tripled in value between 1982 and 1987. You didn't have to know much about which stock to pick or when to buy or sell. You just had to be there.

Is It Worth It?

A successful lawyer who has worked hard for fifteen years and has also had his luck in the market, says his life isn't very exciting. "If you'd told me back then that I'd be making $500,000 a year by the time I was forty I would have pictured a lifestyle of the rich and famous," he says. "But it's nothing like that. My life isn't any more exciting than my friends who make a quarter of what I do. In fact, my life is duller because I'm working all the time. Who are these people I see on TV who look like they have such a terrific life? Skiing, windsurfing, going to parties with fantastic friends, surrounded by beautiful women? Why isn't my life like that? I'm young and healthy and rich. How much do these people make who enjoy life so much? A million a year?"

Achieving financial security, even at a relatively early age, is often a disappointment when too much is expected from money to begin with. As we've noted in this book, too many people never feel secure enough with their money to enjoy it, no matter how much they have.

And as we've just pointed out, the cost of pursuing money is rarely cheap. "I hear a lot of guys my age say they wish they'd spent more time with their kids, had a better marriage, learned how to do this or that," says a retired businessman. "But I don't hear any of them saying they wish they'd spent more time at the office."

It's safe to say that not many people think much about their net worth on their deathbed. Yet so many of us spend the majority of our youth and energy pursuing the dollar as if its accumulation were the most important thing in life and use wealth as the principal measure of our achievement. So many of us believe in that fantasy of money's magic, that it will transform us and protect us. The bind is a difficult one: not meeting money goals when we think of them as very important can be a real blow to self-esteem; meeting them is often disappointing.

Coming to Terms with Having Enough

Like the ten-year-old boy who fantasizes about being Superman, most adults entertain occasional daydreams of being super-rich. These fantasies can be psychologically revealing if you look at them in detail. They can give you some clues about what "enough" really means to you, a more achievable goal.

First, you have to let yourself have the fantasy. Imagine the power and fun of being really rich, of having all the money

you could ever want. Before you puncture the fantasy with
the horrible thought that it probably will never happen,
examine its details for a moment.

What would be the first thing you would do with the money?
How would your daily life change?
Would your self-image change? In what way specifically?
Would your friends change?
Is there anyone you'd tell off?
How do you think others would treat you?
Is your fantasy filled with people, or with things, or with a
general feeling or tone?
Realistically, how much of the fantasy do you think you could
achieve even without the money?

Most money fantasies can be broken down into two areas:
The first has to do with getting out from under. Getting rid
of. Paying off. Not having to do certain things. That's usually revealed in your answer to the question, "What would be
the first thing you would do?" Whatever your financial albatross is, you'd get rid of it. The loan from medical school.
Your $10,000 in credit card debt. Those daunting tuition
bills. Taking a lower-paying job to avoid that god-awful com-
mute. Whatever it is, most of us have something that's a
chronic backbreaker, and that's the first thing our fantasy
takes care of.

Ask yourself—or your spouse, friend, or financial adviser—if there's any way to kill off this albatross in reality.
Have you unwittingly set things up so that you're perpetuating a bad situation rather than trying to solve it? Would a
change in your agreement with money help the problem?

The second general area falls under the heading of getting things and acquiring feelings.

High on almost everyone's list is buying things. A big
shopping spree. That house at the beach. Eating in an
expensive restaurant every night for a week. Buying the

fabulous bottle of wine, the cashmere topcoat, the mink. And then there are the feelings: feeling secure at last. Getting some excitement in your life. Meeting new people. Feeling respected, listened to.

Some of that probably doesn't depend on money. If you look at your list closely and think about it in the terms this book has suggested, you may find ways to grant yourself some of your fantasy through emotional means, or by making strategic changes in your life.

Buying things, of course, takes money. Boy, does it ever. But might there be other, less expensive ways of providing the excitement that buying something represents? And the feeling of security. Might your money style have led you to avoid the kind of simple planning that would enhance your sense of financial security? As for respect, could you be overrating the importance of money? Could you be caught in a sort of "Someday Syndrome," using money as a partial excuse for not doing what you want to do?

In this book we have tried to take the fangs out of the money beast, whether they are rooted in emotional conflict or in lack of information. Once defanged, that beast can become a powerful ally. Your beast may be fear, leading to avoidance of the topic and unnecessary poverty. Your beast may be insecurity, leading you to the frenzied pursuit of more money rather than of more important things, like enjoying your work or stabilizing relationships in your life.

We all bring certain conflicts to money. With reason, insight, and knowledge those conflicts can be resolved so that money can become the simple and useful tool it ought to be. We have tried to show you ways in which you could be happier with money. From pointing out psychological conflicts that may stand in your way, to suggesting practical financial options, we have stressed that you can be the master of your money. In a sense, almost everyone's money fantasy is the same, and it comes down to one word: more.

189

Throughout this book we have suggested ways to change that word to another word: enough. While "more" is an ever-receding goal, "enough" is much more likely within your reach if you clear out the emotional obstacles and systematically pursue it.

ABOUT THE AUTHORS

EDWARD M. HALLOWELL, M.D., is an instructor at the Harvard Medical School and Massachusetts Mental Health Center and is in private practice in Cambridge, Massachusetts.

WILLIAM J. GRACE, JR., is a vice president of Merrill Lynch in Washington, D.C., an active private investor himself, and the author of two successful books on finance.